# Vegetarian
# Cuisine
### from the
# Himalayan
# Foothills

Pahadi karela and coconut

# Vegetarian Cuisine
## from the
# Himalayan Foothills

FLAVOURS AND BEYOND

## Veena Sharma

NIYOGI
BOOKS

Published by

## NIYOGI BOOKS

D-78, Okhla Industrial Area, Phase-I
New Delhi-110 020, INDIA
Tel: 91-11-26816301, 49327000
Fax: 91-11-26810483, 26813830
Email: niyogibooks@gmail.com
Website: www.niyogibooksindia.com

Text © Veena Sharma
Photographs © Nandita Singh, unless otherwise mentioned

Editor: Sukanya Sur
Design: Nabanita Das
Cover Design: Kaushikee

ISBN: 978-93-89136-75-3
Publication: 2021

Printed at: Niyogi Offset Pvt. Ltd., New Delhi, India

Mind, dear boy, is made up of food, prana is made up of water, and speech is made up of fire.

—Uddalaka Aruni to Svetaketu in<br>*Chandogya Upanishad*, 6.5.4

One cannot think well, love well, sleep well, if one has not dined well.

—Virginia Woolf, *A Room of One's Own*

# Contents

# Foreword

Is Veena Sharma's delightful book an artist's cookbook, a yeoman's manual, or a chef's chapbook? It is actually none of these as its value ranges far beyond these binaries.

Through her culinary forays and concoctions, Veena Sharma tries to join and connect rather than separate or divide. As she says in her Entrée, through food and its links to the soil, the sun, and the wind, we make a connection with the cosmic whole.

Seers of India used negatives (*neti neti*) to describe the Ultimate Self. In fact, the Entrée, penned by the author, brings to mind ancient rishis even more vividly. The *Katha Upanishad*, for instance, says the path to the Self is only for the brave-hearts who dare to walk on razor's edge! But don't be alarmed. Her razor-sharp sensibility is used only to dice up the cornucopia that comes from Uttarakhand, that proverbial 'Land of the Gods' (*Deva Bhumi*).

The fusion of food with culture lends itself to another Indic insight: that of food as the Supreme Principle (*Annam Brahma*). The science of Indian therapeutics (Ayurveda) also makes that pragmatic connection.

Food was also deployed as medicine and it became an ornament of cultural traditions. It is in the latter spirit of food as one of the epicurean glories and goals of human accomplishment that Veena Sharma approaches her recipes. Gathered with love and care that is due to preserving a priceless but all too perishable legacy, what a feast for the senses the author has laid out.

Needless to add, her life story is as colourful as the scrumptious spread of her recipes. She headed the Swahili Service of the External Services Division of All India Radio. Widely travelled, she has several books and monographs to her credit. She was also the Founder Chairperson of Prajna Foundation for Cultural Interaction and Studies.

She has now chosen to give up life in the metropolis and live in Rishikesh. Inevitably, Veena Sharma's mouth-watering recipes draw upon local bounties from the Himalayan heights - grains and greens, nuts and fruits - all prepared in time-honoured ways that are slowly being lost or forgotten.

Just peep into her granary: it is bursting with hemp, flax, unhulled local sesame, *tor*, *kulath*, *bhatt* (white and black), *Harsil ke rajma*, *jakhiya*, *faran*, and *chora*. When you couple these grains and seeds, with local leaves, textures, and consistencies lovingly prepared in traditional ways, you end up with myriad paths to gastronomic nirvana, literally on every page.

In all this, even the tiniest seed from the hills comes with its own halo of magical tales: consider just one example of the non-cereal *rajgira* (amaranth); did you know this was originally a gift of the Aztec nation? Having mistaken its local use for anti-Christian ritual, Spanish conquistadors tried to ban its cultivation. But the locals would not listen.

Amaranth happens to be one of the most efficient 'green machines' on earth. It is as easy to grow as pigweed. Meanwhile, captivated by its gold-green foliage, the Spanish took the plant around the world as an ornamental one.

Nobody knows how and when it landed in India, much less about its journey to the Himalayas. Our farmers christened it *ramdana* (god's grain) and *rajgira* (royal grain). The rest is culinary history!

Western science discovered amaranth's secret only in 1956; it is loaded with the essential amino-acid lysine. Combine *rajgira* with corn or wheat, and you get a protein balance much superior to meat and milk.

This brings us to the crucial concept of balance, which lies at the heart of this little gem of a book. 'The moment the body is supplied with the right balance of nutrients, vitamins and minerals the mind becomes light and ready to delve into its own stories,' she writes in her invocation of wholesome foods.

With her abiding interest in the Ayurvedic tradition, and holistic living, Veena Sharma's delectable spectrum of recipes necessarily looks upon the kitchen as the 'best pharmacy'. And her sane advice is that our home pharmacy can provide 'particular admixtures and combinations that would help uplift both our physical and mental constitutions.'

If we but knew what to ingest, and when, she adds, we would be infused with sacred healing that makes our bodies light, and minds sharp. To concur with her sentiment, let's say, '*Tathastu* (So be it)!'

In conclusion, we do hope this foreword has sharpened your appetite, whether to dig deep or lightly, into the 'moveable feast' that awaits you, dear reader, in the pages that follow.

Vithal C Nadkarni
Former Science Editor &
Consulting Columnist
*The Times of India* group

# Entrée

This is a homegrown cookbook, which evolved out of my life experience while playing with flavours and a whole range of palates. It is meant for the bravehearts who wish to explore and create their own range of tasty and nutritious foods, as they connect to the environment and nature.

One of the things that changed when I moved to my little apartment in Rishikesh was my relationship with food. Rishikesh provided me the ambience for reaching out to foods in a holistic manner. As I started cooking, I began to connect to the produce, to the soil, the sun, the wind that nurtured the produce, which in turn nurtured my body and mind. I began to feel that I belonged to a larger whole. Preparation of food became like preparation of oblation and offering for a yajna[1]. A yajna that was performed by the gastric fires within my body, even without my being conscious of it. Every morsel that went into the mouth was like a channelling in of the energy of mother earth and the environment, both of which were inhered by the same vitality. Food became a bridge between the outer macro and the individualized micro worlds that form us. I began to, more and more, see it as a gift of nature that nurtures the reservoir of life force within. I realized that when correctly understood, food could help release the healing processes that the body is naturally endowed with.

The many-textured local grains, lentils, nuts, and seeds that enticed with their shapes and colours encouraged me to explore into their nature, and their connection with me. Seeds, lentils, and herbs like hemp, flax, unhulled local sesame, *tor, kulath* or *gehet, bhatt* (both white and black), *Harsil ke rajma, jakhiya, faran, chora*, and many others called out to be brought into my kitchen, and slowly I began to realize their special benefits for the body, which in turn is deeply connected to the mind. The flours available - anything from *mandua* (a local finger millet), *rajgira* (amaranth) and local soya, to *jhangora*, bajra or jowar or local corn - provided gluten-free nourishment that also resulted in shedding

---

1   The word 'yajna' refers to a sacrificial fire in which offerings are made to the gods, elements, or planets for general benefit.

Fresh farm produce

excessive weight. The rare spices, rare not only because they are not seen so commonly outside of these regions[2] but also because they grow in remote altitudes, also called attention.

Every season presents crops that are specific to that time. With the onset of the monsoon, many kinds of greens start appearing in the market. Their leaves, textures, and consistencies, when cooked, are different to those of the summer vegetables. And when the monsoon is over, the markets are flooded with other varieties - amaranth, mustard, *rai*, *pahadi palak*, *bathua*, and many interesting vegetables.

There is a surfeit of shops carrying holistic foods of different kinds, as Rishikesh has become a hub for the new-age seekers of spirituality who jostle with traditional pilgrims. Those enticed by yoga practices look for food that would cleanse their overloaded systems. The coming of the Beatles in the 1960s is now looked upon as an added attraction for the town, especially for those from outside the country. Organic and health food shops abound in the area for these explorers

who come for an overhauling of the body. So, even though the infrastructure of the place leaves much to be desired, people still feel something special in the energy that permeates the region. The requirements of the incoming floating population have given rise to high-quality facilities standing directly adjacent to highly neglected spaces that send out urgent SOS signals for attention.

Besides, there is now an emphasis on Rishikesh being an adventure destination. The Ganga is not just the holy river to be worshipped as the Mother, she is also the carefree, hazardous waterway that must be approached with respect and caution. Rafting and various related enterprises have sprung up around the river. As such, it is not just the devoted faithful but the adventure lovers as well that are drawn to the place. As a result, there is much experimentation in the field of cuisine. Small cafes and kitchens here serve more wholesome foods than is found in most metropolitan cities.

Then, there are the convenience foods that cater to indigenous pilgrims and tourists. We see roasted corn on cobs, toasted local sesame, and puffed amaranth seeds turned into easy to eat forms, often combined with *gud*. There are also the ubiquitous puffed rice and roasted chanas. Several seeds make for nutritious dishes, especially during times of fasting, of which there are many in the course of the year. Piles of coconuts, with their husks looking like peaked

---

2   In most cities and towns several grocery shops nowadays carry off-the-beaten-track items. Navdanya may also have a presence in different parts of the country.
We suggest the following online resources:

1. Himalaya 2 Home | himalaya2home.com
2. Uttarakhand Foods | uttarakhandfoods.com
3. Samaun - The Himalayan Treasure | samaun.com
4. Himjoli - Treasures of Uttarakhand | himjoli.org

Indigenous *gud* (jaggery) fabrication
*Photo: Vikram Sharma*

caps, abound for the ritualists who come to offer sacrificial prayers.

Coming up to Rishikesh by road, I have been drawn by the indigenous fabricators of *gud* – that wonderful golden cake-like confection made from fresh sugarcane juice. Its texture, colour, and taste is so much more wholesome than the unappetizing cold grains of white sugar. *Gud*, 'without chemicals', is something that I have to compulsively pick up before reaching Rishikesh. Entering the town, one encounters a plethora of sugarcane juice vendors with bundles of sugarcane reed ready to be put through their hand-operated juice wheels for the tired and thirsty.

The feel and texture of the ingredients gives pleasure to the senses of taste, sight, and smell. The sensations of sound and touch are not left out either, as the sizzles and splutters that accompany the use of these ingredients having different consistencies cater to those as well. The colours and beauty of the produce have encouraged me to grow some small plants and herbs on my balcony. The fragrance and energy exuded by their varied hues and shapes, and their wisdom regarding when to bloom, when to fruit, and when to hold back beckons me as I look out of my window.

I had always felt that one's kitchen could be one's best pharmacy, providing us with the particular admixtures and combinations that would help uplift both our physical and mental constitutions. If we knew what and when to ingest certain foods into our systems we would be infused with sacred healing that would make our bodies light and minds sharp.

The moment the body is supplied with the right balance of nutrients, vitamins, and minerals, the mind becomes light and ready to delve into its own stories. (The temporary giving up of certain grains and the consumption of certain seeds and nuts during days of ritual fasting helps accentuate such combinations.) The key is to experiment and, in the process, find the balance. The *Chandogya Upanishad* says that the mind is made up of food. So I feel every morsel feeds my personality, as personality is nothing other than the thoughts the mind brings up. Thus, to some extent, my relationship to food also becomes responsible for my thoughts! In Sanskrit there is a saying, *ahara shuddhau sattva shuddhih*, that is to say wholesome food leads to a good mind. As such, the Hindi aphorism, '*jaisa anna vaisa man*', meaning 'you are what you eat' or rather 'you think as you eat' is not an off-hand remark.[3] Science of physiology tells us that our brains, accounting for 2 per cent of body weight take up 20 per cent of the nutrients we consume. The transfer of energy from food to neurons in

---

3   Hippocrates, the Greek physician of 5th millennium BC, is said to have declared, 'Let food be thy medicine and medicine be thy food,' establishing the link between food and the body-mind complex.

the brain plays an important role in our cognitive abilities. Thus, food impacts our capacity of retention, recall, alertness, and mental stamina.

A simple story in the *Chandogya Upanishad* narrates how a father carries out an experiment on his son, who is also his disciple. He tells the son to refrain from eating for fifteen days. He was allowed to drink any amount of water and, of course, breathe the pure air of their home! After fifteen days, when the father asks him to recite from the Vedas, the boy is unable to recall anything. Thereupon, he is advised to go and eat. After that, the boy is able to recite whatever the father asks him to. This is meant to establish the direct relationship of food with the mind.

Due to my never-throw-away-anything mentality, my food has the quality of a mélange. From this tendency arise creations that come as a surprise. I do not feel restrained due to not having this or that ingredient. Something else always serves the purpose and, at times, brings out more interesting and delectable results, leaving people guessing what it was that had been used. Rishikesh further lifted the sense of restraint, as I felt like experimenting with many of the unfamiliar-looking ingredients that I had not encountered before.

I have never been a scientific cook. Almost never does a dish come out looking or tasting exactly the same, as though out of a food factory. Yet, it carries an 'almostness' which gives it an added excitement. It tastes good and carries with it an experimental, explorative quality, evoking a sense of 'I-can-do-it-too' in the eater. But it also makes me a little suspect, as many are the times when people ask me for a recipe and I am at a loss to provide one as they are made up of a little-bit-of-this and a little-bit-of-that, and 'why-not-this-also' which gives an under-probation quality to my food. At times, people think I do not want to divulge the recipe, even though I am happy to share. It became easier when Nandita came forward and volunteered to help with measurements and act as a kind of scientific lab assistant. Her questions about the quantity and the reason for a particular ingredient helped my own clarity with regard to what I did non-consciously earlier.

I also do not like to labour for hours over a particular dish, even though I like it to be presentable and enjoyable. So what we tried were mainly recipes that were fun and easy to prepare and did not take too much time. I found that it was possible to use the local ingredients in ways that suited the urban table, and actually added to it nutrients that had slowly become marginalized due to the unrestricted use of refined products. Besides, these ingredients expand our personalities as they stretch them out to connect with the environment that sustains and forms us.

Himalayan grains and seeds—kale bhatt, kulath, rajma, and masoor

# Introduction
### The Sacred Land: A Culinary Smorgasbord

It is not for nothing that the Garhwal region of the Himalayas is referred to as *deva bhumi*, the land of gods. The topography and climate of this sacred land has spawned a rich biodiversity of flora and fauna, which is a natural heritage of the area. Water currents carrying rocks and herbs, fed by high-altitude minerals and vegetation irrigate the soils. Steep hillsides etched by terraced farms and, fed by mountain streams produce crops suited to their particular terrains. The diversity of crops resulting from the variations in elevation, differences in orientation and gradient, as also the velocity of winds and quality of precipitation they are exposed to is what gives to this area its environmental uniqueness.

The different crops provide rare nutrients that cannot be obtained from any single crop. Relying on elements such as sunlight, biomass from forests, and crop residues, farmers here have traditionally worked from an understanding of the ecological principles that underlie natural phenomena, to grow crops suited to their specific area. Respect for, and a connection with nature has led to the emergence of many important religious shrines along the confluences of major tributaries of the sacred river Ganga.

Since the choice of the food we eat is influenced and determined by the society and culture we live in, food in these hills, till recently, had not been driven by fashion or commercialization. For millennia, these hill people lived on whole grains and unprocessed fresh produce. Being connected to nature and the environment, they consumed that which nature provided in different times of the year, as that is what the body requires in those seasons. A combination of natural whole foods and physical exertion in this undulating region is what traditionally gave these people their sturdiness. Hill women are slender and strong as they move up and down the slopes like mountain goats.

Today, our 'technologically advanced' society has introduced abundant and easily available packaged, preserved foods that often call for no preparation. Heavy with unwanted fats and carbohydrates, these 'empty foods' result in the overfed and undernourished persons we encounter, especially in metropolitan areas. The hill people are also becoming victims of the smart inroads made by these foods resulting in sluggishness and uncalled-for fatigue, dull hair and skin, and other troublesome afflictions that can often be traced back to the food consumed.

Perhaps, it is a recognition of this fact that is turning our gaze on ancient grains and herbs that have nourished societies since millennia. We are well aware that macronutrients - carbohydrates, proteins, and fats - give us energy, build muscle, and strengthen our physiological equipment, which are necessary for the efficient functioning of our minds and bodies. But we often do not give enough attention to micronutrients - the vitamins, minerals, fibres, and trace elements - that are essential for the metabolization and absorption of the macros for their optimal functioning and becoming suitable for our bodies. Macronutrients are like fuel, which demands a clean and greased engine for proper combustion. Micronutrients are the grease and oil that not only maintain the cleanliness and smoothness of the engine, but actually break down the heavy macronutrients so that

our bodies may absorb them easily. So, it is not just what we put into our mouths but how we process it that matters.

Our finely tuned bodies do not absorb macronutrients in the form they are received. Rather, by a complex metabolic process, they first break them down to their molecular forms and then *re-form* them into subtler varieties of carbohydrates, proteins, and fats - like amino acids, fatty acids, and glucose. These are the forms in which these nutrients are received by the trillions of super-microscopic cells and tissues that our bodies are made up of. It is the minute micronutrients that enable this breakdown of food, which otherwise would either pass out of the system undigested or block some of the subtle passages and cavities causing unwanted deposits. Micronutrients are what combine with the numerous bodily secretions and catalyse chemical reactions to promote 'communication' among the millions of cells, and enable the subtle nutrients to reach where needed, and/or make up a deficiency of one by taking up and converting energy from another. So, there is a riotous intelligent activity of breaking down, reconstitution, and absorption ceaselessly raging within our systems. The better supplied our system is, the more efficient this activity.

No one food can give us all the multitudes of micronutrients that are required for the breakdown and release of the macros. Hence, the need for diverse foods that Nature, in her abundance, supplies us with at different times of the year. While macronutrients can be stored in the body for some time, the delicate micronutrients have to be supplied regularly. The hills abound in seasonal foods that provide these nutrients according to the needs of the body, enabling it to cope with different requirements – keeping it hydrated in summer, warm in winter, etc.

Classically, we eat to gain energy and build our bodies. But we also eat for pleasure. Eating is the most satisfying activity we undertake, as food caters to a deep-seated human craving. When cravings, motivated by commercial pressure, take over, we tend to lay stress on certain foods at the expense of others, ignoring the nutrients that our superiorly operating bodies demand. The minute cells and nerve tissues are the foremost sufferers in this process, as the gross foods are not transformed into subtle forms for transportation and absorption into our ultra fine crevices due to lack of consumption of micronutrients. It is, perhaps, these artificial cravings (or just thoughtlessness) that deprive our tables of the numerous natural textures and colours that are often the indicators of the nutrients those foods carry.

The science of Ayurveda informs us that there is a connection between what we eat and how we act or behave. Our food has an impact on our sense of well-being and harmony, as also our levels of aggression and depression, and, of course, satisfaction. So not only at the individual, but at the societal level also, food tends to have an impact on our interactions.

Ayurveda tells us that just as our physical constitution is characterized by different proportions of *vata* (air), *pitta* (heat or fire), and *kapha* (viscosity or water), we also have a corresponding mental constitution determined by the qualities of *sattva*, *rajas*, and *tamas*. A balance of the three is required for normal functioning in the world. Each personality is made up of a different balance of these qualities. The balance needs to be maintained for a creative and harmonious functioning at the individual and societal levels.

On the physical side, *vata*, the mobile energy and life force of air and ether, governs movement, including the flow of breath, pulsation of the heart, muscle contractions, and cellular mobility. It promotes the faculty of communication by strengthening the mind and the nervous system. It is, thus, linked to creativity and flexibility, as also levels of anxiety and overactivity. As a general rule sweet, sour, and salty food cooked with ghee and served warm suits the *vata* element.

*Pitta*, carrying the healing and transformative energy of heat, governs digestion as it sustains metabolism and body temperature.

It is related to intelligence, understanding, thoughts, and emotions. It also engenders physical and psychological endurance. Pungent and bitter foods, ripe fruits and vegetables cooked in less oil regulate *pitta*. Sour food may not be too appropriate for the *pitta* constitution.

*Kapha*, the viscous and binding energy reserve of the body, being associated with the earth and water elements, lends structure, solidity, and cohesiveness to the body. It hydrates the cells, lubricates the joints, and moisturizes the skin. It also helps maintain immunity and protect body tissues. Equated to the watery energies of empathy and compassion, it creates a sense of peace and patience to sustain consistent effort. It is perhaps also conducive to good sleep. The sluggishness of *kapha* is pacified with pungent, bitter, and astringent food using a minimum of oil and fat. Mucous-provoking food could aggravate this element.

On the mental side, *sattvic* personalities display greater creativity and mental and physical alertness. They remain enthusiastic with regard to what they undertake and are able to solve life's problems more easily. They display a cheerful and serene countenance, and do not suffer from mental fatigue even after working mentally for long hours. *Sattvic* food is light, unctuous, and packed with nutrients. Milk, butter, ghee (clarified butter), fresh and dried fruits like almonds, dates, lentil sprouts, and whole grains, and a number of seasonal vegetables contribute to this type of personality. Gourds of different kinds are also suited to this type. Spices used in *sattvic* cooking include turmeric, ginger, cinnamon, coriander, fennel (*saunf*), cardamom, and several digestive herbs.

*Rajas* is characterized by an aura of restlessness. *Rajasic* personalities tend to be somewhat ambitious, aggressive, and competitive. There could even be a tendency in them to control others. On the hand, *rajas* provides energy to perform and actualize the creativity of the *sattvic* mind. *Rajasic* personalities favour food that is oilier and spicier as compared to *sattvic* food. They prefer foods that are bitter, sour, salty, pungent, hot, and comparatively dry.

*Tamasic* personalities are generally depressive and sluggish, given to much eating and drinking. A little mental work tires them easily. *Tamasic* food is generally overcooked, preserved and processed – food made from refined flour (*maida*), pastries, pizzas, burgers, chocolates, soft drinks, tea, coffee, tobacco, alcohol, canned and preserved food like jams, pickles, and fermented food, fried food, ice creams, puddings, and a number of 'fun food' are unfortunately included in this list. The good news is that when freshly prepared at home with wholesome ingredients, these same foods can provide fun as well as nourishment!

SATTVA

BEINGNESS
HARMONY
LIGHT
PURITY
RIPENESS
BALANCE

RAJAS

MOVEMENT
ACTION
ENERGY
CHANGE
RAWNESS
CREATIVITY

TAMAS

SLUGGISHNESS
INERTIA
DARKNESS
HEAVINESS
STALENESS
MATERIALITY

Gunas and the human personality

As there is an absence of micronutrients in *tamasic* food, they leave us with a sense of non-satiety even after we have eaten a full meal. This is because the body secretes a number of juices and enzymes to mingle with micronutrients to help the breakdown of larger foods. When those are not supplied, there is a sense of craving and one puts in more of the same kind of heavy food, stretching the stomach walls, burdening the digestive system and retaining a sense of dissatisfaction. Overstretched stomach walls can also impact the functioning of the heart and lungs, which share the same general space.

Too much *rajas* or *tamas* can have a negative impact on our lives. A balance of all three is what makes up an efficient and healthy mind. As such, a combination of varied foods to cater to the differing needs of the body at different times is needed. In a well-balanced system, the digestive fires would further 'cook' the foods to draw out their optimal nutrients.

I felt that the several prescribed days of fasting in this area (these days are also known in other parts of India, but perhaps observed more avidly here) are an important contributor to physical and mental well-being. Our rubber-ball-like stomachs, normally about the size of our fists, stretch to accommodate the food we put into it, which in three to five hours is pushed out to other parts of the digestive tract. During days of fasting, by either refraining from food

Haldi has antioxidant properties

or eating limited quantities of light food, we allow the stomach to rest, become empty, and regain its natural contour and size. That is the time when we experience 'real' hunger as against craving. With a little sensitivity and observation, as also experimentation, we can train our brains to signal 'real' hunger as against 'nutritional' hunger that manifests as craving.

Consequently, it is worth investing a little time and resources in the quality of ingredients and the mode of preparation of food. For, that goes a long way in determining the health of the molecules, those microscopic constituents that carry nutrients to every cell and tissue in the inmost recesses of the body and determine the state of our bodies and minds.

# Legumes

For healthy hearts and heads

The diverse terrain of Uttarakhand is home to a number of legumes rich in nutrients. Legumes consist of peas, beans, peanuts, soyabeans, and lentils. No local meal is complete without some form of legumes - the unpolished red, brown, green, and black varieties in their natural hues. Unrefined grains retain more nutrients as compared to their refined versions. Being rich in minerals like iron, manganese, phosphorus, potassium, fibre, and proteins, legumes help maintain overall health and boost the immune system. They have been crucial in creating the sturdy physiques of the hill people, who have traditionally worked hard on the lands. Legumes are also environmentally friendly as they help the growth of other crops by leaving behind nitrogen that enriches the soil to feed other plants.

Even so, there can be no food that is perfect in itself. All foods carry some elements that are unfavourable for the human system. It is the way it is prepared and combined with other ingredients that makes a particular food suitable for human consumption. With all their beneficial qualities, legumes also carry a toxin called lectin, which if not cooked properly can cause symptoms such as upset stomach, diarrhoea, bloating or abdominal discomfort, and fatigue. Too much lectin irritates the intestinal lining. It can, thus, cause muscle and joint pain, and also brain fog. As such, some people are known to be averse to legumes.

Lectins are supposed to have evolved as a natural defence system in plants to deter fungal growth and prevent pests, insects, and animals from eating the seeds and plants. Since a seed is meant to grow and create a plant, and does not want to be consumed by some other living species, it creates its own protective armour in the form of lectin. That is what prevents it from breaking down too easily. Cooking, sprouting, or fermenting legumes deactivates and greatly reduces their lectin content, making them fit for human health.[1]

By the same token, lectins, in small quantities, are known to have some health benefits, as they set into motion antimicrobial and anti-tumour activities in the colon.

While some legumes like kidney beans are heavy on lectins, most lentils - red, brown, green, black, or yellow - are softer and lighter on the system. Easier to digest, they form an important source of protein, iron, and vitamins of the B group. An important micronutrient that all legumes contain is a soluble fibre called prebiotic. Prebiotics travel (undigested) down the alimentary canal and reach the intestinal tract, where they provide nourishment for the trillions of helpful bacteria and microbes that live inside our systems. These good bacteria produce vitamins and enzymes that assist in digesting and absorbing nutrients, and in fighting harmful pathogens. They also help with removal of toxins and excretion of waste. Thus, prebiotics serve as crucial fodder for the good

microbes. Fibres also help increase the 'satiety' hormones that tell us when we are full. This helps prevent overeating due to craving from lack of nutrients. There are many types of prebiotic fibres, and legumes contain many of them. Dr Denis Burkitt, a British physician who served in Kenya, Somalia, and Uganda during World War II, discovered the importance of fibres in diet. He arrived at the hypothesis that dietary fibre plays a major role in protection against colonic cancers. Working in Uganda in the 1960s, he found that 'many of the diseases that are widespread in Western countries...are absent in the Third World, including appendicitis, diverticulitis, diabetes, heart disease and certain cancers....(This is) due to the way we (Westerners) eat.' Dr Burkitt stressed that common diseases could be prevented, possibly cured, by eating simple, inexpensive foods. Some of his famous quotes state: 'Diseases can rarely be eliminated through early diagnosis or good treatment, but prevention can eliminate disease.' Correct food is the preventive that protects us from disease.

Indigenous Uttarakhandis have evolved their own methods of preparing legumes, so as to draw out optimal nutrients. Taking cues from them, the legumes in the following recipes were cooked in somewhat creative ways that gave them a slightly different look and flavour, making them attractive to cosmopolitan palates.

---

1  It may be mentioned here that some processed foods, especially those containing wheat, corn, and soyabeans, besides containing too much sugar and starch, may be loaded with lectins. And these do not have a chance of being eliminated, as, being already processed, they cannot anymore be cooked, sprouted, or fermented to eliminate those lectins.

# HORSE GRAM KEBAB
## Kulath (gehet daal) ke kebab

PREPARATION TIME: 15–20 MINUTES | COOKING TIME: 15–20 MINUTES | 4–6 SERVINGS

*Kulath* or *gehet* daal is a local favourite and is available in a number of *dhabas* as a main dish to go with rice or *mandua ki* roti. In Ayurvedic medicine, it is seen to have several medicinal qualities. Known to have astringent and diuretic properties, it is believed to be beneficial for treating kidney stones. In case of urinary infection, it is recommended that a person drink the water in which this daal has been boiled, as that helps to clear the urinary tract. Recommended as a treatment against water retention, it also makes for a good weight loss diet. Besides, it helps to lower cholesterol levels!

In local recipes, other than being cooked as a soupy daal, *kulath* is often used as a stuffing in parathas or *kachoris*. In these forms, it also makes for a good breakfast dish. Since those are the known forms, we gave a different twist to the daal by turning it into an appetizer or snack or even a part of the main meal.

❀ Soak overnight
Kulath/gehet daal  **½ cup/ 70 gm**
Split Bengal gram (chana) daal  **½ cup/ 90 gm**

❀ Boil both the daals separately with salt (to taste) since the daals have different cooking times. Start with just enough water and add water, if needed, till the daals are soft and can be easily pressed between the fingers.

❀ Roughly mash the daals together using a potato masher or fingers or just a ladle. The mash will be coarse and there may even be some stray grains left intact.

❀ Add
Freshly chopped coriander  **6 tbsp/ 20 gm**
Ginger  **2 tbsp/ 20 gm**

Chopped green chilli  **1 tbsp/ 5 gm**
Coriander (dhania) powder  **1 tsp/ 2 gm**
Cumin (jeera) powder  **1 tsp/ 2 gm**
Dried mango powder (amchoor)  **1 tsp/ 2 gm**
Black salt (kala namak)  **1 tsp/ 4 gm**
Dates  **5** (soaked in warm water for 1-2 hours, then chopped coarsely)

❀ You may also add
Raisins  **1 tbsp/ 10 gm**

❀ Add

Malai (cream skimmed
off the top of boiled milk) **2 tbsp/ 30 gm**

❀ Mix well. Make flattened rounds, the size of
aloo tikias (about 2" in diameter).

❀ Press both sides into a tray of unhulled
sesame seeds or sprinkle the seeds on them
and press gently on each side. (White sesame
seeds can also be used.)

❀ Cook in a non-stick pan with minimal
sunflower oil, flip when one side looks golden
and crisp.

❀ Cook the other side till crisp.

꙰ Serve with a chutney of choice. Coconut
Chutney (p. 121) may go well with it.

# TANGY PIGEON PEA
## Tor daal

PREPARATION TIME: 15 MINUTES  |  COOKING TIME: 25–30 MINUTES  |  2–4 SERVINGS

Himalayan (*pahadi*) *tor*, called *arhar* in many parts of India, is known to have the ability to control blood pressure, stimulate growth, improve the immune system. Rich in complex fibres, carbohydrate, iron, calcium, phosphorous, magnesium, and Vitamin C, B1, and B9, the daal has traditionally been used in Ayurveda for several purposes. Calcium, phosphorous, and magnesium are known as 'macro minerals', as they are required in larger quantities by the body as compared to iron, copper, zinc, and iodine.

*Pahadi tor* is smaller than the one available in the plains. It is, as such, quite popularly eaten whole, whereas the larger grain is mostly turned into a split form in other parts of India. The split daal form is popularly used in southern Indian dishes like *sambhar*. In northern India, it often goes by the name of yellow daal. I find that the *pahadi tor* has a slightly dry and brackish taste, which gets balanced by the addition of a little tamarind along with other spices.

Being low in calories, it can form a good part of a nutritious weight loss diet.

❀ Soak overnight
Tor daal  **½ cup/ 90 gm**

❀ Cook the soaked daal in pressure cooker
   with a little salt. The daal takes long to
   cook. It may require 5-6 whistles or more.
   Set aside.

❀ Soak in warm water, strain the pulp, and
   set aside
Tamarind  **1" x 1" piece/20 gm**

Drumstick (sehjan)  **1**
❀ Scrape them lightly and cut into 2" pieces.

❀ Heat in a saucepan
Mustard oil  **1 tbsp/ 10 ml**

❀ Add
Wild or dog mustard (jakhiya)  **1 tsp/ 2 gm**

❀ Allow to splutter, then add
Allium/ jimbu (faran)  **1 pinch**
   (Faran, a delicate spice, is added after the
   spluttering of other spices and just before
   the main ingredients.)

❀ Add
Onion finely chopped  **2 tbsp/ 16 gm**
Garlic, finely chopped  **½ tsp/ 2 gm**
Ginger, finely grated  **1 tsp/ 5 gm**
Green chilli, finely chopped  **1**

❀ Add drumsticks (sehjan) and stir well till all
   ingredients are well mixed.

❀ Sprinkle water from time to time and cook
   for 3-4 minutes.

❀ Add
Tomatoes, pureed in a blender
   **4 tbsp/ 60 gm/ 60 ml**

❀ Cover and cook for 5 minutes. Add tamarind
   paste. Mix well and cook for
   2-3 minutes. Add tor daal and cook for
   15 minutes stirring occasionally.

❀ Mix in
Fresh coriander, chopped  **1 tbsp/ 4 gm**

❀ Cook for a minute and serve.

🌿 Serve with rotis or rice.

# HIMALAYAN BLACK GRAM
## Pahadi urad daal

*Chainsoo* made from *urad* daal is a local favourite. It is made by grinding the roasted daal and then cooking it into a thick soup-like consistency. Along with *mandua ki roti* or rice, it makes for a nourishing staple dish. Rich in iron, it helps boost energy levels and keeps one active. The high fibre content - both soluble and insoluble - makes it easy to digest. Besides, it is rich in protein and minerals like potassium and vitamins of the B group. It is also high in iron content. Its regular consumption helps control cholesterol.

I realize *pahadi urad* is softer and cooks a little faster than the regular *urad* we get in the plains, though I did soak this one too, before cooking.

❀ Wash well and soak overnight
Pahadi urad **½ cup/ 100 gm**

❀ Cook in pressure cooker with a little salt, then add
Turmeric (haldi) **¼ tsp/ 1 gm**
❀ In the meantime, heat in a small skillet
Sunflower oil **1 tbsp/ 10 ml**

❀ Add
Wild mustard (jakhiya) **1 tsp/ 2 gm**
Jamboo (faran) optional **few strands**
(Faran is not to be spluttered like jakhiya)
Green chilli, slit **1 whole**
Curry leaves (kadhi patta) **6-8**
Onion, finely chopped **1 tbsp/ 8 gm**
Garlic, finely chopped **1 tsp/ 4 gm**
Ginger, finely chopped **2 tsp/10 gm**

❀ Cook for 4-5 minutes, till onions are translucent. Then add

Fresh tomato puree **2 tbsp/ 30 gm/ 30 ml**

❀ Cook for 5 minutes mixing well. Pour the mixture into the daal and mix well. Add one by one the following ingredients, folding them in and mixing well

Yoghurt (dahi) **¼ cup/ 50 gm/ 50 ml**
Top cream of milk (malai) **¼ cup/ 50 gm**
Himalayan rock salt (saindha namak) **1 tsp/ 5 gm**
Asafoetida (hing) **¼ tsp/ 1 gm**
Fresh coriander (dhania), chopped **1 tbsp/ 4 gm**

❀ Stir and cook for a few minutes. Serve hot.

🍴 Serve with rice or rotis.

## RICE BEAN DAAL
Riyaans daal (*Vigna umbellata*)

PREPARATION TIME: 20 MINUTES | COOKING TIME: 25–30 MINUTES | 2–4 SERVINGS

Among the lesser known daals is the Himalayan *riyaans*, a small kidney-bean-like legume. It is made up of a number of rainbow-like hues, as beans on the same plant carry different colours. Hence the name *navrangi* daal. *Navrangi* daal is a rich source of proteins, vitamins, fibre, minerals, and carbohydrates. Its various curative properties include its value for diabetic and heart patients. It is both a low cholesterol and a low-fat food.

The taste of *riyaans* is very different from that of kidney beans, even though they resemble each other. One finds that tamarind (*imli*) or mango powder (*amchur*) cuts through the brackish taste, as it does with *tor*, and helps release the nutrients. We prepared it in a simple way and it came out to be delicious.

❀ Measure
Rice beans (riyaans) **½ cup/ 80 gm**

❀ Soak overnight and then cook in a pressure cooker till soft. The daal takes long to cook.

❀ In a pan, heat
Mustard oil **1 tbsp/ 10 ml**

❀ Add
Wild mustard (jakhiya) **1 tsp/ 2 gm**
Dry red chilli **1 whole**
Onion, finely chopped **1 tbsp/ 8 gm**
Garlic, finely chopped **1 tsp/ 4 gm**
Ginger, grated or chopped **1 tbsp/ 10 gm**

❀ Let these cook till golden.

❀ Add
Turmeric (haldi) **½ tsp/ 1 gm**
Chora (liqourice-like stick), crushed **1" stick**
Cumin (jeera) powder **½ tsp/ 2 gm**
Coriander (dhania) powder **½ tsp/ 1 gm**
Himalayan rock salt (saindha namak) **1 tsp/ 5 gm**

❀ Add the cooked riyaans. Add more water, if needed, to keep a gravy-like consistency.

❀ When the flavours are blended, add
Tamarind (imli) paste **1 tbsp/ 10 gm**

❀ The paste can be prepared by soaking the tamarind in hot water for about half an hour and then rubbing through a fine sieve.

❀ Add
Jaggery (gud), finely grated **1 tbsp/ 8 gm (or less)**

❀ Bring to a boil and serve garnished with green coriander or fresh marjoram, or cherry tomatoes.

It pairs well with rice but can also be had with rotis.

# KIDNEY BEANS FROM HARSIL
## Harsil ke rajma

PREPARATION TIME: 15–20 MINUTES | COOKING TIME: 20–25 MINUTES | 2–4 SERVINGS

Kidney beans or rajma come in many forms. Each one has its own flavour and specialty. *Harsil ke rajma* grow in a small area in the upper reaches of Uttarakhand. They usually come into the market around the month of October. They have an off-white pinkish hue and are a little flatter then the red kidney beans. They are softer than many other types of rajma, so they cook faster as compared to them. A simple preparation retains their original flavour and creaminess.

❀ Soak overnight in a little water
Kidney beans (rajma) **½ cup/ 80 gm**

❀ Cook in a pressure cooker with a little salt
   and turmeric (haldi), till 3-4 whistles.

❀ In the meantime, heat in a skillet
Oil **1 tbsp/ 10 ml**

❀ Add
Dried red chilli **1**
Curry (kadhi) leaves **few**
Wild mustard (jakhiya) **½ tsp/ 1 gm**, let splutter
Beefsteak plant, *Perilla frutescens*
   (bhangjeera, optional) **½ tsp/ 1 gm**
Onion, finely chopped **1 tbsp/ 8 gm**

❀ Add and cook till translucent
Ginger, finely grated **1 tsp/ 5 gm**
Coconut, grated **1 tsp/ 3 gm**

❀ Cook for a few minutes till lightly browned
   and add to the cooked rajma.

❀ Then add
Fresh tomato puree **2 tbsp/ 30 gm/ 30 ml**

❀ Close the lid and cook a little more till soft
   and creamy.

⚑ Rice may be a preferred companion to Rajma,
   but rotis can also be served with it.

# Seeds & Herbs

## Til, jakhiya, chora, faran
### (Sesame, dog mustard, angelica, allium)

L to R: Sesame, dog mustard, angelica, allium

One of the oldest oilseed crops, sesame (*til*) is very much in the picture in Garhwali cuisine. The unhusked dark variety (these are different from the black *til* used for offerings in temples) is commonly seen in many shops. High in energy due to their oil content, the seeds are rich in many vitamins of the B group. They are also known to be a rich source of calcium, magnesium, phosphorus, and zinc. The dark seeds contain good quantities of iron. I found a good variety of dark *til* sold by a vendor in Dev Prayag where the river Alaknanda joins the river Bhagirathi to formally 'launch' the river Ganga. The seeds went a long way in enriching our food – both in palatability and nutrition. They are locally available in most shops.

When not available, the white husked variety may be used with good effect.

Growing in the wild, at heights of 500 to 1500 metres, *jakhia*, a delectable and popular spice, is also called 'Garhwali jeera', though it is not like *jeera* at all. The English term for this seed is possibly 'dog mustard'. The

A jakhiya plant.
Image Source: Jeevan Jose / Wikipedia / CC BY-SA 4.0

naturally in the upper regions of the Himalayas, this bark-like spice (that looks a little like the liquorice stick) has a flavour-enhancing quality. When crushed and added to any daal or long-cooking vegetable, *chora* plays a role in enriching their natural flavours, as also providing its own earthiness to the dish. It has many digestive qualities and may help reduce bloating of stomach caused by certain food.

Found in the high altitudes of the Himalayas, *faran* (also known as *jimbu*), which belongs to the allium group is a sought-after garnish. The saffron-like strands that are supposed to belong to the onion family are known to be a blood purifier and very beneficial for digestion and common cold. The herb is available at certain times of the year, but the strands dried in the shade have a good shelf life. Even so, it is not always easy to find. Some online vendors sell it.

locals use this smaller-than mustard seed as a spice for tempering many daals and soft, watery vegetables like gourds. The pungent and crunchy flavour is more delectable than *jeera* or even mustard seeds. Like many of the seeds and herbs found in the region this, too, has several medicinal qualities. It has certain wound-healing qualities, as it helps reduce inflammation and swelling. Besides, it is said to be good for the liver.

Another local spice that one is initiated to by local shopkeepers is *chora*. Growing

# Vegetables
## Greens that keep the body moving

Vegetables may include leafy greens, roots, and tubers, or may appear as different-shaped protrusions in varied colours in different plants. Containing little carbohydrate and very little protein, they are rich in vitamins, minerals, and fibre. As such, they are a panacea for keeping off unnecessary weight. Combined with legumes and cereals, these make for a wholesome diet, as it is these micronutrient-rich foods that enable the carbohydrates and proteins of the former to break down and become suitable for the body. Every vegetable has its own unique property, which may even serve as a medicine for some specific diseases.

A large variety of vegetables appear in the markets at different times of the year, marking the seasons like summer, monsoon, autumn, or winter. While the summer months bring up succulent and juicy vegetables, it is in the winter that the abundant green leaves that form a powerhouse of iron, vitamins, and minerals make their appearance. Amaranth, *bathua* (*cheel bhaji* or lamb's quarter), mustard (*sarson ka saag* in North India), spinach (*palak* in North India) of different varieties, *methi* (fenugreek), and greens from radish, beetroot, turnip abound in the market. Each comes with its own particular flavour, adding to the variety of tastes, textures, and colours, as also nutrients to the table. The number of hues that the colour green boasts may come as a surprise.

Since the needs of the body vary according to the climatic conditions, nature provides vegetables and other produce according to those needs. That is why it is recommended that we consume that which grows in a particular season. This would also minimize the consumption of frozen and stored produce even while giving us what we need at a given time. There is a good reason for the nine days (Navaratri) of fasting twice in a year at the time

Bhindi (okra) is rich in fibre

bacteria but enable efficient movement of food through the intestinal tract, where absorption, as well as elimination of toxins and residual food takes place. Fibres help to strengthen nerve fibre and tone muscle fibre. The soluble variety of fibres helps to break down nutrients into subtle forms acceptable to the brain. It is significant that the gut is called the 'second brain'. The phrase 'gut feeling' comes from the special capacity of the gut to *think* on its own. As such, fibres, by maintaining a clean gut, play a role in resisting age-related mental disorders such as dementia and depression. Since the brain consumes a vast amount of energy compared to the rest of the body, the mechanisms involved in the transfer of energy to brain cells is instrumental to brain function. Soluble fibres enable this process.

Insoluble fibres, on their part, act as a broom or a scrub for the gut, as they help push out waste. They assist with better absorption in the intestinal tract by helping to keep it clean.

of changing seasons, once in spring and then at the onset of the winter season. The fasting period - in which light foods are consumed - helps to prepare the body for the changing climatic and food conditions it is about to face. In the springtime, the body gets ready for the juicy and cooling summer food. At the onset of winter, it is prepared to take in warming and energizing products that winter brings.

A very important component of almost all vegetables is fibre. Fibres are carbohydrates that the body cannot digest, but they help digest other foods and keep the system running smoothly! Fibres, both soluble and insoluble, play a major role in the metabolic processes in the body. Also known as roughage, they not only feed the good

# HIMALAYAN SPINACH WITH DRUMSTICKS
## Pahadi palak aur sehjan

PREPARATION TIME: 20 MINUTES | COOKING TIME: 10 MINUTES | 2 SERVINGS

The deep green leaves of *pahadi palak* are smaller than those of the spinach found in the plains. I found it to be more palatable as it carries a slightly sour taste and is less acidic in its effect as compared to the large-leafed *palak*.

*Palak* is rich in folate or folic acid (also found in orange juice and yeast). The liver also generates several forms of folate after the intestine absorbs sufficient quantities of vitamin B. Folate deficiency, which is mostly caused by low dietary intake, is associated with a number of physiological abnormalities. Adequate levels of folate are essential for brain function and its deficiency can cause neurological disorders, such as depression and cognitive impairment. Consumption of folates, especially in conjunction with vitamins of the B group can be effective in preventing cognitive decline and dementia.

Steam and puree in the mixer Himalayan
   spinach (pahadi palak) **1 cup/ 250 gm**

❀ Heat
Sunflower oil **1 tsp/ 5 ml**

❀ Add to it
Cumin (jeera) powder **½ tsp/ 2 gm**
Green chillies, slit **2 whole**
Onion, finely chopped **1 tbsp/ 8 gm**

❀ Cook for 1-2 minutes. Then add
Garlic, finely chopped **½ tsp/ 2 gm**
Drumsticks, cut into 2" pieces **1**

❀ Stir and cook for a few minutes, then add
Fresh tomato puree **4 tbsp/ 60 gm/ 60 ml**
Ginger, finely grated **1 tsp/ 5 gm**

❀ Sprinkle water as and when required.
❀ Let it cook for 5-7 minutes till drumsticks
   are soft.
❀ Add the pureed spinach (palak) and
raisins **1 tbsp/ 10 gm**

❀ Add salt to taste. Cover and cook for a few
   minutes. Add water if needed, but serve it
   reasonably dry.

❀ Serve with rice or rotis.

# BOTTLE GOURD WITH COCONUT AND POPPY SEED
## Khus-khus aur nariyal ki lauki

PREPARATION TIME: 15–20 MINUTES | COOKING TIME: 20–25 MINUTES | 2–4 SERVINGS

Bottle gourd or *lauki* is a water-filled summer vegetable that keeps the system cool and hydrated, replenishing the loss of fluids through sweat and heat. Bottle gourd is a rich source of vitamin C, A, E, and K and calcium. It is also rich in iron, folate, potassium, and manganese. Some people drink its juice first thing in the morning for its blood sugar and blood pressure regulating qualities. It is also helpful in alleviating intestinal tract infections. The essential nutrient, choline, in it helps improve brain function and reduce stress and depression.

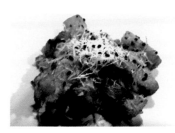

❀ Lightly roast, separately
Freshly grated coconut **2" square/ 25 gm**
Dried red chilli **1 whole**
Poppy seeds **2 tsp/ 6 gm**
❀ Set these aside

❀ Heat
Oil **½ tsp/ 3 ml**

❀ Roast till nicely golden brown
Onion, finely chopped **1 tbsp/ 8 gm**

❀ Blend all the roasted ingredients into a mealy, crumbly powder and set aside.
❀ Heat in skillet
Peanut oil **1 tbsp/ 10 ml**

❀ Add
Wild mustard (jakhiya) **1 tsp/ 2 gm**
Bottle gourd (lauki) cut into small cubes
    **2½ cups/ 250 gm**

Turmeric (haldi) **½ tsp/ 1 gm**
Salt **to taste**

❀ Cook for a few minutes till the gourd is sautéed.
❀ Add the crumbly powder and mix well, coating the gourd evenly.
❀ Add
Water **2 tsp/ 10ml**

❀ Continue cooking till tender (add more water, as needed; some bottle gourds release more water than others).
❀ Then add
Jaggery (gud) **1 tsp/ 4 gm**

❀ Stir well and cook for a few minutes. You may sprinkle some toasted pumpkin seeds on top before serving which will add to the crunchy flavour.

🌿 Serve with plain chapatis.

# SWEET AND TANGY PUMPKIN
## Khatta-meetha kaddu

PREPARATION TIME: 15–20 MINUTES | COOKING TIME: 20–25 MINUTES | 4 SERVINGS

Pumpkin, a ubiquitous vegetable, seems to be available all the year round and almost everywhere. It comes in many different colours and shapes. It allows itself to be used in a variety of ways. I like to use the yellow variety, as it has a rich texture that goes especially well with puris.

High in vitamins A and C, pumpkin is also a good source of potassium and magnesium. Its comparatively high carbohydrate content, which may not be very agreeable to persons inclined to diabetic conditions, can be countered with spices like fenugreek. Other than combining different tastes, Ayurveda also recommends that it is important to consume a variety of colours. Each colour has its own therapeutic value that goes into strengthening the system in different ways. The yellow and orange food groups, such as papaya and carrots, are generally high in beta carotene and carbohydrates. The carotenoids therein are converted by the system into vitamin A and antioxidants that help fight cancer, as also keep the skin and eyes healthy. These foods help protect the digestive membrane, to some extent preventing ulcers and acid reflux.

❈ In an open pressure cooker, heat
Mustard oil **1 tbsp/ 10 ml**
Dry red chilli **1 whole**
Yellow mustard seeds **½ tsp/ 1.5 gm**
Black mustard seeds **½ tsp/ 1.5 gm**
Fenugreek (methi) seeds **1 tsp/ 4 gm**
Nigella sattiva, black seeds (kalonji) **1 tsp/ 2 gm**

❈ Let them splutter. Then add
Unpeeled diced pumpkin (it may be
lightly scraped to remove any adhesions) **350 gm**

Turmeric (haldi) powder **½ tsp/ 1gm**
Salt **1 tsp/ 4gm**

❈ Stir and cook for about 6-7 minutes. Then add
Dry mango (amchoor) powder **½ tsp/ 1 gm**, or more
Dry ginger powder/saunth **1 tsp/ 1 gm**

❈ Close the lid and allow to cook till two
   whistles. Let it cook in its own steam and
   open when all the steam has escaped. After
   opening the cooker, add
Jaggery (gud), grated **1 tbsp/ 8 gm**

❈ Cook for a few minutes till the jaggery is
   well harmonized with the pumpkin. This goes
   very well with puris. A dish of potatoes tossed
   with tomatoes (tamatar aloo, p. 49) may be
   added as a further accompaniment with the
   puris.

# GREEN PEAS WITH CREAM
## Matar malai

PREPARATION TIME: 5 MINUTES | COOKING TIME: 20–25 MINUTES | 2–4 SERVINGS

The winter season brings in mounds of tasty green peas. Try to get large quantities of them when they are at their best; shell and freeze them in small packets to be used during seasons when variety in vegetables becomes highly reduced. A home in the Himalayan foothills lends access to the best crop of fresh seasonal fruits and vegetables, which can be stored for lean days. The high fibre content of peas helps regulate bowel movement. Besides, they are high in Vitamin K, which enables the anchoring of calcium in the bones, reducing the risk of osteoporosis.

Like some of the legumes, peas nourish the soil in which they grow by drawing nitrogen from the air and fixing it in the soil. After harvest, the remaining part of the plant breaks down to form a natural fertilizer for the soil.

Shelled peas (matar) **1 cup/ 140 ml**
❀ Cook with ¼ cup water and mash lightly. Adjust the water to allow it to reach a semi-mashed consistency, not too soft. Set aside.

❀ In a skillet, heat
Peanut oil **1 tbsp/ 10 ml**

❀ Add
Wild mustard (jakhiya) **1 tsp/ 2 gm**
Green chilli **1 whole, slit**
Yellow mustard seeds **½ tsp/ 1.5 gm**
Brown mustard seeds **½ tsp/ 1.5 gm**

❀ Let the seeds splutter. Add
Red onion (chopped) **1 small/ 16 gm**

❀ Sauté till golden brown. Add the mashed peas and cook over low heat, adding a little water to keep it moist. Cook for about 15 minutes. Then stir into the mixture
Fresh cream (malai) **2 tbsp/ 30 gm**

❀ Cook till heated and well-blended. Take it off the stove. Serve warm.

✿ Serve hot with plain paratha or chapatis.

# PEAS AND DRUMSTICKS
## Matar sehjan

Peas can be prepared in a number of ways. They also pair well with other vegetables. Here, we put them together with drumsticks (or *sehjan*), the long chewy pods of the tree, *moringa oleifera*. It is a popular ingredient in many parts of India. A superfood, it is used extensively in herbal medicines also. All parts of the moringa tree have some medicinal and nutritional properties. Moringa powder made from dried and powdered moringa leaves has become a popular food supplement. It is rich in various antioxidants, including quercetin and chlorogenic acid. Moringa leaf powder can increase blood antioxidant levels. The long pods with the young seeds inside have many health benefits. High in fibre content, they induce good sleep, and regulate blood sugar levels. The leaves are also a great source of iron, protein, and vitamins A and C. They reduce joint pains, lower cholesterol, promote heart health, and induce the death of cancer cells.

Fresh shelled peas (matar) **1 cup/ 140 ml**
Drumstick **1** (lightly scraped into 2" pieces)

❀ Heat
Oil **1 tsp/ 5 ml**
Dried red chillies **2 whole**
Curry leaves (kadhi patta) **5-6**
Wild mustard (jakhiya) **1 tsp/ 2 gm**

❀ Let it splutter.

❀ Add peas and sauté for a couple of minutes.
❀ Sprinkle water and cook till the peas become half tender. Then add
Fresh ginger, grated **1 tsp/ 5 gm**
Fresh tomato puree **2 tbsp/ 30 gm/ 30 ml**
Turmeric (haldi ) **½ tsp/ 1 gm**

❀ Add tender drumsticks. Sprinkle some water. Cover and cook while stirring occasionally, adding water as and when required. The vegetables should be moist with just a little water in them. Add
Beaten yogurt (dahi) **3 tbsp/ 40 gm**

❀ Mix in yogurt a minute before taking off the stove and stir well.

❀ A raita on the side could enhance the dish.

# TOMATOES WITH HIMALAYAN POTATO
## Tamatar aloo

PREPARATION TIME: 10 MINUTES | COOKING TIME: 20-25 MINUTES | 4–6 SERVINGS

Another dish that goes well with puris or parathas is this one made out of *pahadi* potatoes, which have a thin skin and a fluffier texture than some other sticky varieties.

Potatoes are among the most consumed food items the world over and also serve as 'comfort food'. Easy to digest, they are high in roughage and facilitate the movement of food through the system. Their potassium, magnesium, phosphorous, and zinc contents are good for the skin. Even the water in which potatoes have been boiled or washed is good for the skin.

The addition of dried fenugreek leaves (*kasoori methi*) in this dish not only adds to the flavour and taste; it is also beneficial for those suffering from diabetic problems. It helps regulate cholesterol levels in the body.

Himalayan potato (pahadi aloo) **500 gm**
- ❀ Steam the potatoes, with their peel till soft. Cool and lightly remove peel. Let some peel remain, as it adds to the flavour and nutrition. Press the potatoes between the palms of the hands to roughly break them up. Set aside.

- ❀ In a pan, heat
Pure ghee **1 tbsp/ 10 ml**

- ❀ Then add
Dried red chilli **2 whole**
Wild mustard (jakhiya) **1 tsp/ 2 gm**
Black mustard seeds **½ tsp/ 1.5 gm**
Yellow mustard seeds **½ tsp/ 1.5 gm**
Nigella sativa (kalonji) **1 tsp/ 2 gm**
Fenugreek (methi) seeds **1 tbsp/ 8 gm**

- ❀ Allow all of these to splutter, then add
Jimbu (faran, p. 38) **10-12 strands**

Pureed fresh tomato **500 gm/ 2¼ cup**
Crushed stick of chora **½ " stick**
- ❀ Simmer till tomatoes lose their rawness, then add
Asofoetida (heeng) **a pinch**
Dried fenugreek leaves (kasoori methi) **2 tbsp/ 2 gm**
Grated jaggery (gud) **1 tbsp/ 8 gm**
Turmeric (haldi) **½ tsp/ 1 gm**
Himalayan rock salt (saindha namak) **1 tsp/ 5 gm**

- ❀ Add the roughly crumbled potatoes. Stir well and let cook till potatoes are steeped in the sauce. Keeping them for a while before serving would help the sauce to seep into the potatoes.

- ❀ This goes well with puris or parathas.

# GOLDEN WHOLE POTATOES
### Chatpata aloo ka chokha

**PREPARATION TIME: 10 MINUTES | COOKING TIME: 25–30 MINUTES | 4 SERVINGS**

A delicious preparation of small potatoes that goes well with all breads. To get vitamins B and C, as also the iron from it, potatoes should be consumed whole - the flesh as well as the skin. The peel carries nourishing fibre, and is a richer source of iron and fibre than the flesh. It also contains greater amounts of magnesium and potassium that carry electrical charges, which stimulate muscle contraction and help transmission between nerve cells.

Potatoes (small) **12** (about 1" or more in diameter)

❀ Wash them well. Remove any dirt and damaged peel, keeping as much of the peel as looks clean and fresh. With a small sharp fork, pierce the potatoes on all sides to allow the spices to penetrate when cooking.

❀ Heat
Oil **1 tbsp/ 10 ml**

Dried red chilli **1 whole**
Black mustard seeds **½ tsp/ 1.5 gm**
Yellow mustard seeds **½ tsp/ 1.5 gm**
Wild mustard (jakhiya) **1 tsp/ 2 gm**

❀ Add the pierced potatoes and let them be well-coated with the oil and spices. Then add
Turmeric (haldi) **1 tsp/ 2 gm**
Himalayan rock salt (saindha namak)
   **1 tsp/ 5 gm (to taste)**
Cumin (jeera) powder **1 tsp/ 2 gm**
Coriander (dhania) powder **1 tsp/ 2 gm**

❀ Sprinkle water from time to time. Cover and let them cook. When soft (it may take a while depending on the potatoes), add
Dried mango powder (amchoor) **1 tsp/ 2 gm**
Ginger powder (saunth) **1 tsp/ 1 gm**

❀ Heat some more till the spices are well-blended.

🍃 Date chutney (p. 124) would go well with the potatoes.

# SWEET POTATO AND PLANTAIN MASH

## Kachhe kele aur shakkarkandee ka chokha

**PREPARATION TIME: 15–20 MINUTES | COOKING TIME: 20–25 MINUTES | 4–6 SERVINGS**

The idea evolved from the ubiquitous street-food vendors who roast the sweet potato (or even *kachaloo*, a variety of yam) on charcoal fire and serve it sliced with some savoury spices (masala) on it. In our recipe, we added plantains for an extra dose of potassium and other nutrients, and mashed the two into a hummus consistency. The two together blend well and provide a good dose of vitamins A, C, and B. Plantains caught our attention as they could be seen growing in many places around our residency complex.

❀ Steam
Sweet potatoes **2 (medium sized)**
Plantains **2 whole**

❀ When soft, mash the two together (the plantain was peeled, but much of the sweet potato skin was left on for its potassium and fibre content) and add spices of choice.

❀ Add
Chaat masala **1 tsp/ 2 gm**
Fresh lemon juice **1 tsp/ 5 gm**
Himalayan pink salt **½ tsp/ 2 gm**
Black salt **½ tsp/ 2 gm**
Red chilli powder **¼ tsp/ 1 gm**
Roasted ground cumin **½ tsp/ 2 gm**

❀ A little extra lemon juice can be added to increase the vitamins and flavour. Top each serving with
Dry roasted mixed seeds **¼ tsp/ 1 gm**

❀ A mixture of seeds from pumpkin, cucumber, melon, and a swirl of olive oil may be used.
❀ This can be served as a first course appetizer, or as part of the main meal, or as a snack with afternoon tea, or even as a dip.

# FENUGREEK LEAVES WITH COTTAGE CHEESE
## Methi paneer

PREPARATION TIME: 15–20 MINUTES | COOKING TIME: 15 MINUTES | 2–4 SERVINGS

This brings in the much-needed bitter taste to the table. The dark green *methi* (fenugreek) leaves, with a grassy and sweetish aroma, are somewhat bitter in taste. The bitterness mellows when cooked. Fenugreek blends well with other foods. Dried or fresh fenugreek is often added to parathas and rotis for added flavour and nutrition. The seeds go a long way in adding flavour to varied foods.

Fenugreek leaves have a high water content and contain good amounts of vitamin C, potassium, and iron. They are also high in soluble dietary fibre, which helps lower blood sugar.

The bitterness can be reduced by sprinkling the leaves with a little salt, letting them stand for a while, and then squeezing out some of the water before cooking.

As for paneer, I use that which I prepare at home. In Rishikesh, we have a choice of either double-toned milk, which is very watery, or a rich full-cream milk that provides a thick layer of cream after it is boiled. I remove the cream and use it in other recipes, and use the de-creamed milk for preparing paneer.

❀ Steam with a little water, puree, and set aside.
Fresh fenugreek (methi) leaves **1 cup/ 75 gm** washed and chopped.

❀ To make paneer, bring to a boil
Milk **2 cups/ 450 ml**

❀ Add to the boiled milk
Vinegar **1 tbsp/ 10 ml**

❀ Mix the vinegar with
Water **1 tbsp/ 10 ml**

❀ The milk will separate. If required, add a little more vinegar to make sure that the water separates completely. Let simmer for a few minutes till the paneer coagulates. It does not require stirring.
❀ Strain coagulated paneer, drain any excess water, and keep aside. Press it under a heavy pan, letting the residual water drain out. It can then be cut into rough squares. (The water from the paneer makes a good addition to gravies, daals, and soups.)

❀ In a skillet, heat
Sunflower oil **1 tbsp/ 10ml**
Whole cumin (jeera) **½ tsp/ 1 gm**
Slit green chilli **1 whole**

Split Bengal gram (chana) daal **1 tsp/ 4 gm**
Split pigeon pea (arhar daal) **1 tsp/ 4 gm**
Grated fresh ginger **1 tsp/ 5 gm**

❀ Let the daals sautee till a bit browned.

❀ Mix in pureed methi. Add
Paneer water (drained from the paneer) **¼ cup/ 110 ml**
Turmeric (haldi) **½ tsp/ 1 gm**
Himalayan rock salt (saindha namak) **½ tsp/ 2.5 gm**
Jaggery (gud), grated or crushed **2 tsp/ 8 gm** (more jaggery may be added if required)

❀ Roughly slice paneer into small cubes and add to the methi.
❀ Mix gently for a couple of minutes. Finish off with
Lemon juice **1 tsp/ 5 ml**

❀ Stir and serve.

**Note**: Instead of steaming and pureeing the fenugreek leaves, one can also chop them very fine and cook them with the dry spices till the leaves are nicely browned and then add the cottage cheese. This may give it a crispier texture.

✦ Serve hot with parathas or plain chapati.

# ZUCCHINI AND SWEET POTATOES TOSSED IN MUSTARD SEEDS AND POPPY SEEDS

## Bhuni turai aur shakkarkandee, khus-khus aur sarson ke daane se

PREPARATION TIME: 15–20 MINUTES |
COOKING TIME: 20–25 MINUTES |
4–6 SERVINGS

Nandita, my photographer, tried out a dish by placing some zucchini slices on mustard seeds heated in a little oil in a skillet and allowed them to cook on one side till browned. When done on one side, she turned them to brown the salted other side as well. The simple dish was delectable even as it retained the natural flavours of the zucchini.

Taking a cue from that, I sprinkled a mixture of mustard and poppy seeds on a skillet with the barest touch of oil and placed on it the zucchini slices. Then I sprinkled a little Himalayan salt on the open side and let cook till the underside was slightly caramelized by the vegetable's own sweetness. Next, I flipped it for the salted side to cook. I did the same to steamed sweet

potatoes cut into round slices. Served with a chutney or a dip, they make for a wholesome addition to the main meal.

Zucchini **1 medium** (sliced)
Sweet potatoes **2** (steamed lightly and cut into ¼" thick, round slices)

❀ Heat oil in a large skillet
Sunflower oil **3 tsp/30 ml**
Yellow mustard seeds **1 tbsp/6 gm**
Black mustard seeds **1 tbsp/6 gm**
Poppy seeds (khus khus) **1 tbsp/6 gm**
Himalayan pink salt **to taste**

❀ Sprinkle some of the seeds in very little oil. Small quantities of seeds will be needed at one time, as all the slices of the zucchini or sweet potato cannot be done at the same time and the process will have to be repeated.
❀ Place slices of zucchini and then sweet potato into the seeded oil. The seeds will stick on that side.
❀ The two should be done separately as they require different durations to cook.
❀ Dust the exposed upper side with salt. Flip when one side is nicely caramelized (from the vegetable's own juices) and repeat for the other side. No need to put more seeds for the other side.
❀ To give a little crunch to this dish, serve it with a semi-dry chutney (see the chutney section p. 117).

# PLANTAIN AND SAGO (TAPIOCA) CUTLETS

## Kachhe kele aur sagudane ki tikia

PREPARATION TIME: 15–20 MINUTES  |  COOKING TIME: 20–25 MINUTES  |
6–8 SERVINGS

While the starchy sago does not have many vitamins or minerals, or proteins and fats, it is a soothing and easy-to-digest food that helps settle bile-related problems, which can cause abdominal discomfort. It is also rich in antioxidants and fibres that help ease out toxins from the body. It is used during fasts in the form of a *khichri* or even as kheer when boiled in milk. In Ayurvedic terms, it is seen to be a cooling food that helps calm the gastric fires. I have used it with plantains, which grow quite abundantly in our residency complex and on the hills around, to get a rich combination of nutrients that would be easy to digest. Plantains, a superfood in themselves, are rich in complex carbohydrates, vitamins, and minerals and, like sago, are easily digestible. They form a staple food for millions of people in several parts of the world. They are also an important source of magnesium and potassium. Their fibre content helps the bowel to move.

Unlike dessert bananas, plantains must be cooked before they are consumed.

Tapioca (sago, well-soaked in water) **¾ cup/120 gm**
Plantains **5**

- ❀ Always soak tapioca in water for 4-5 hours or even longer. The longer it is soaked, the easier it is to cook the translucent pearly balls.
- ❀ Steam the plantains in pressure cooker with their peels on.
- ❀ Remove peel and mash the flesh when cool. Add the soaked sago along with
Onion, finely chopped **2 tbsp/ 16 gm**
Fresh ginger, finely chopped or grated **1 tbsp/ 10 gm**
Green chilli, finely chopped **1 tbsp/ 5 gm**
Garlic, finely chopped (lahsun) **1 tsp/ 4 gm**

Ground coriander (dhania)  **1 tsp/ 2 gm**
Ground cumin (jeera)  **1 tsp/ 2 gm**
Dried mango powder (amchoor)  **1½ tsp/ 3 gm**
Ginger powder (saunth)  **1 tsp/ 1 gm**
Lemon juice  **1 tsp/ 5 ml**
Lemon rind  **½ tsp/ ½ gm**
Salt  **to taste**

⊛ Form the mixture into small round cutlets or *tikia*s. Press them into finely spread-out sesame seeds and pan fry with 1 tsp oil in a non-stick pan. Serve with your favoured chutney (p 119).

# STIR-FRIED GREEN PLANTAIN
## Kacche kele ki sukhi sabzi

PREPARATION TIME: 15–20 MINUTES  |
COOKING TIME: 10 MINUTES  |  4–6 SERVINGS

Plantain is rich in complex carbohydrates, vitamins, and minerals and is easily digestible. It is also an important source of magnesium and potassium. The fibre content in plantains eases bowel movement and helps keep the system clean.

❀ For this dish, lightly steam
Plantains **3 whole**

❀ The plantains are to be steamed with peels till they are not too soft. The peel needs to be lightly scraped before steaming to remove grit and to also get rid of some of the tough fibre.
❀ After steaming, cut them into ¼" thick slices (along with the remaining peel).
❀ Place these in a skillet and add
Oil **1 tsp/ 10 ml**

❀ Sprinkle the slices with Himalayan rock salt to taste and add
Turmeric (haldi) **½ tsp/ 1 gm**
Ground cumin (jeera) **¼ tsp/ 2 gm**
Ground dhania (coriander) **¼ tsp/ 1 gm**
Ginger powder (saunth) **¼ tsp/ a pinch**
Dried mango powder (amchoor) **¼ tsp/ ½ gm**
Kashmiri red chilli for colour and flavour **¼ tsp/ a pinch**

❀ Stir till the plantains are well-coated with the masala and the slices are soft and creamy. Serve hot.

❧ Can be served as a snack or with the main meal.

# JACKFRUIT BONANZA
## Mazedaar kathal

PREPARATION TIME: 15–20 MINUTES | COOKING TIME: 20–25 MINUTES | 4–6 SERVINGS

The largest tree-borne fruit, *kathal* or jackfruit is looked upon as fruit by some and as a vegetable by others. Some jackfruits can be as large as three feet long! The ripe fruit has a strong odour, but when cut up and eaten, it has a sweet creamy taste. Green jackfruit, mostly used in the northern part of India as a vegetable, has a neutral taste and goes well with other vegetables and spices. My Uttarakhandi helper makes a delicious pickle (*achaar*) from the vegetable.

The fleshy fibrous fruit in its raw form is a rich source of carbohydrate, and vitamin B6. It is, of course, rich in dietary fibre and hence very good for the alimentary system. It also contains some amounts of vitamin C and potassium.

❀ Roast separately, grind together, and keep aside
Red chillies **2**
Poppy seeds (khus khus) **1 tbsp/ 6 gm**
Fresh ginger, finely cut or grated **1 tbsp/ 10 gm**

Jackfruit (kathal), cut into cubes **250 gm**, roast separately

❀ The fibrous portion will stick out from the cubes. Pan-fry the cubes in a little oil till lightly brown. Keep aside. It is best to have the jackfruit peeled by the vendor as the thick skin is prickly and exudes a sticky juice that is a bit hard to get off the fingers.

❀ In a pressure cooker, heat
Oil **1 tbsp/ 10 ml**

❀ Add
Onions, finely chopped **1 tbsp/ 8 gm**
Green chilli, slit **1**
Salt **to taste**

❀ Add the prepared jackfruit (kathal). Then add
Turmeric (haldi) **½ tsp/ 1 gm**
Coriander (dhania) powder **½ tsp/ 1 gm**
Cumin (jeera) powder **½ tsp/ 1 gm**
Chora **½" stick**
Faran pinch of
The poppy seed (khus khus) mash **full portion**

❀ Stir well till the spices are well-blended. Add a little water, close the lid, and let cook till 2-3 whistles. Open the cooker after it is cooled. Add
Tomato, freshly pureed **6 tbsp/ 90 gm/ 90 ml**
Jaggery (gud), grated **1 tsp/ 4 gm**

❀ Close the lid and cook it again till tender.

❀ Serve with paratha or plain chapati.

# HIMALAYAN BAMBOO SHOOT
## Himalaya ke baskeel

**4–6 SERVINGS (FOR BOTH)**

It was during the rainy season that some neighbours of my Uttarakhandi helper went foraging in the forest for fresh, cone-shaped bamboo shoots. They gave some to her.

The shoots had to be treated before they could be used in any cooking. So the raw shoots were peeled, slit into long fine slices, and boiled in water to which was added a little salt and ash from burnt wood to help soften it and rid it of toxins and any bugs.

The wood ash gave it a smoky flavour. (Commercially available canned shoots already have their toxins removed.)

This seasonal delicacy is rich in the B-complex group of vitamins such as thiamin, riboflavin, niacin, and vitamin B-6. The shoots also contain good amounts of minerals, such as manganese, potassium, and copper, as well as small amounts of calcium, iron, and phosphorous.

The shoots are cooked using two methods.

## First method

**PREPARATION TIME: 5 MINUTES |**
**COOKING TIME: 10 MINUTES**

✾ Heat
Oil **1 tsp/ 5 ml**

✾ Add to the hot oil
Green chilli, slit **1**
Onion, chopped fine **1 tbsp/ 4 gm**
Fresh ginger, grated **1 tbsp/ 10 gm**

✾ Let the onions brown lightly. Then add
Prepared bamboo shoot (baskeel) **2 cups**
✾ Add salt to taste and let cook. Then add
Freshly pureed tomato **½ cup/ 100 gm**

✾ Cook till the tomato is done.

## Second method

PREPARATION TIME: 10 MINUTES |
COOKING TIME: 5 MINUTES

❊ Lightly roast
White sesame seed **1 tsp/ 7 gm**
Poppy seed (khus khus) **1 tsp/ 3 gm**

❊ Blend in coffee grinder and add
Sweet basil leaves (murua) **6-7**
Green chilli **2**

❊ Heat in a skillet
Oil **1 tsp/ 5 ml**

Whole cumin (jeera) **1 tsp/ 2 gm**

❊ Add to this
Prepared bamboo shoot (baskeel) **2 cups**

❊ Stir and add the ground seeds and leaves.
Add salt to taste. Stir till the bamboo shoots
are well-coated in the spices and are lightly
cooked.

✻ Bamboo shoots can make a good addition to a
pasta dish.

# HIMALAYAN BITTER GOURD
## Kakora / pahadi karela

**PREPARATION TIME: 10 MINUTES | COOKING TIME: 10 MINUTES | 2–4 SERVINGS**

Karela or bitter gourd is a very beneficial vegetable, but due to its bitter taste it is not the most popular. Karela is a highly recommended vegetable for those suffering from diabetes, as it regulates blood sugar levels. It is also a great blood purifier. Karela is generally available in summer. But there is also another version, one that is seen during the rainy season. *Kakora, kantola,* or *pahadi karela* is a sweet and very delectable version of the vegetable. It is a thorny, bright green, loquat-shaped vegetable, attractive to look at. *Kakora* is supposed to have many cancer-fighting elements. Rich in fibre, it is also beneficial for preventing ailments related to the eyes and heart. It is useful in fighting coughs and colds in times of changing weather. It is aslo known to have some anti-allergic and analgesic ingredients. In season, it is recommended that *kakora* be consumed at least three to four times a week. The vendor told me that it should be cooked simply, after scraping off the outer thorns.

Himalayan bitter gourd (kakora) **250 gm**
❀ Scrape clean the thorny outer growth and split each piece lengthwise into two.

❀ In a skillet, heat
Oil (I used organic coconut oil) **1 tbsp / 10 ml**
Green chilli, slit lengthwise **2**
Wild mustard (jakhiya) **½ tsp / 1 gm**

❀ Let it splutter, then add
Himalayan sesame (pahadi til) **½ tsp / 1 gm**
(White sesame can be used if the other is not available)

❀ Add the slit kakora
Salt **to taste**

Turmeric **½ tsp / 1 gm**
❀ Stir to get the vegetable evenly coated in the spices. Then add
Powdered cumin **½ tsp / 1 gm**
Powdered coriander **½ tsp / 1 gm**
Stir and let it cook till tender.

❀ Some of the pieces may have rather large fibrous seeds, those can be removed if preferred. It takes a few minutes to cook and needs almost no water. My experimental dish was much liked and was finished in no time.

⚘ As this bitter gourd is not bitter it can be paired with a meal of daal and rice.

The hills, dales, and mountains of Uttarakhand abound in leafy greens that can prove to be an elixir for life. Many of the Himalayan saags or the leafy greens, like different types of spinach, mustard, *chaulai* (amaranth that sets the mountains ablaze with its red blooms), and *methi* are popular names. There are others that are lesser known but have potent healing and nourishing powers. Nettle, the stinging *bicchu buti*, is seen to have many life-sustaining qualities. The 12th-century Tibetan saint, Milarepa, who lived in various caves in the region of Mount Kailash, clad in just a cotton cloth, lived for long periods on just nettle broth. Practising some breathing exercises that helped keep the body warm at heights of 17,000 ft to 19,000 feet, the saint lived till the ripe age of 85 years.

Then there are the large-sized leaves of the turmeric plant, which are used to wrap certain foods for steaming. In the process, the leaves induct their medicinal qualities into the food that is cooked in them. There are also the large leaves of the *arvi* (colocasia) plant, which are often cut fine and turned either into a kofta form or kneaded into flour for making rotis. I also tried some *rai*, *poi*, *chaulai* (amaranth), and *lingdaa* leaves to great advantage.

# BROWN OR CHINESE MUSTARD LEAVES
## Rai

PREPARATION TIME: 10 MINUTES | COOKING TIME: 15–20 MINUTES | 2 SERVINGS

The science of Ayurveda lays great stress on balancing the six tastes of sweet, sour, salt, pungent, bitter, and astringent in our food. My Bengali music teacher, Sri Panchanan Sardar, used to insist that a bitter dish has to be a part of every midday meal. Many winter leaves provide us the slight bitterness required to provide this balance and facilitate secretions of different digestive juices. Rai leaves, somewhat similar to mustard greens, are one of those ingredients. They are prepared simply.

❀ In a skillet, heat
Mustard oil **1½ tsp/ 15 ml**
Wild mustard (jakhiya) seeds **1 tsp/ 2 gm**
Faran **a pinch** (add after the jakhiya has spluttered)
Finely chopped ginger **½ tsp/ 5 gm**
Dried red chilli **1**
Finely chopped fresh mustard (rai) leaves
   **2½ cups/ 200 gm**
Salt **to taste**
Turmeric (haldi) **½ tsp/ 1 gm**

❀ Sprinkle some water and cover, turning them around occasionally till cooked. Then add
Grated jaggery (gud) **1 tsp/ 4 gm**

❀ Mix well while cooking on slow fire.

⚘ Serve hot with rice or roti, and perhaps some yoghurt or raita on the side.

# VINE SPINACH OR MALABAR SPINACH
## Poi

PREPARATION TIME: 15 MINUTES | COOKING TIME: 15 MINUTES | 2 SERVINGS

I found the vine spinach (*poi ka saag*), also known as Malabar spinach, in the monsoon season. There are a few varieties of *poi*. I found two. The vine carrying a purple stem and deep green leaves is pleasing to look at. This is a succulent saag that has a viscous sap. The viscous mucilage is known to be a particularly rich source of soluble fibre. The mucilaginous texture, very different to the other saags that we are used to, is good for the intestinal lining. It is also high in vitamin A, vitamin C, iron, and calcium. Low in calories, it is high in protein.

Vine spinach (poi saag) **1 bunch, approx 250 gm**

⊛ Separate the stems and leaves. Chop the stems finely. Cut the leaves not as finely as the stems.
⊛ Cook the stems for a few minutes in
Oil **1 tsp/ 5 ml**

⊛ Together with
Dry red chillies **1-2**

⊛ Then add
Finely chopped onions **1 tbsp/ 8 gm**
(a few more may be added if liked)

⊛ When the stems are slightly soft (they don't take too long to cook), add the chopped leaves and cook the two for another few minutes.
⊛ Add
Turmeric (haldi) **½ tsp/ 1 gm**
Himalayan rock salt **to taste**

⌇ The saag tastes delicious when served with fresh rotis or parathas.

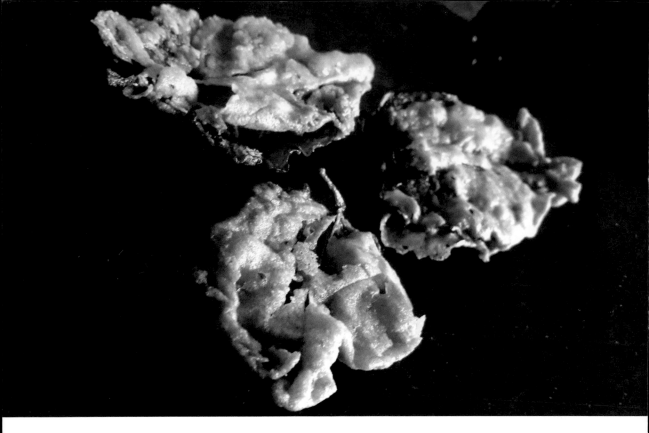

# SPINACH FRITTERS
## Poi ke pakode

PREPARATION TIME: 5 MINUTES | COOKING TIME: 5 MINUTES | 2 SERVINGS

I used some of the whole leaves to prepare the *poi ke pakoras*. For this, I cleaned the leaves in clean running water and prepared a batter to dip the spinach leaves before frying.

❀ The batter is made from
Chickpea flour (besan) ¼ cup/ 25 gm
Carom or bishop's weed (ajwain) ¼ tsp/ 1 gm
Red chilli powder ¼ tsp/ 1 gm
Himalayan rock salt ½ tsp, or to taste

❀ Slowly add water while stirring and getting a thick custard-like consistency. Then dip the leaves one by one in this batter and fry them in ¼" depth of oil placed in a skillet. The leaves, being fleshier than spinach, hold well and make for fresh, crisp pakodas.

This is served as a snack or even as a side dish with soup.

# AMARANTH LEAVES
## Chaulai

This ancient superfood is used both in its leafy form as also in its seed form. In both forms, it is full of calcium, protein, and amino acids. Like other green leaves, it carries different types of fibre to enable better absorption of nutrients. The seed – known as *rajgira*, meaning 'royal food' – is used either as flour, or toasted or popped or sprouted for different preparations. The seeds are popularly used during times of ritual fasting, and some preparations also make good travelling companions. The leaves, when in season, make a wonderful *saag*.

The amaranth leaves have been cooked in this recipe in a way somewhat similar to *poi*.

Amaranth leaves (chaulai), finely chopped
**1 bunch, about 300 gm**

❀ Heat in a skillet
Oil **1 tsp/ 5 ml**
Wild mustard (jakhiya) seeds **½ tsp/ 1 gm**

❀ Let it splutter. Then add the following
Chopped amaranth (chaulai)
Finely chopped onion **1 tsp/ 4 gm**
Finely chopped ginger **1 tsp/ 5 gm**
Salt **to taste**

❀ Turn off heat when the leaves look well cooked. They can be turned into a dry, well-fried bhujia or left semi-moist. A bit of jaggery (gud) may be added while it is still warm and just before serving the dish.

꙳ Most saags go well with bajra or makki ki roti.

# FIDDLEHEAD GREENS
## Lingdaa

PREPARATION TIME: 10 MINUTES | COOKING TIME: 10 MINUTES | 2 SERVINGS

*Lingdaa*, found in the monsoon season like *poi*, also falls in the category of saags. The peculiar appearance of *lingdaa* attracted my attention as I was exploring the vegetable market during the rainy season. The bright green fronds open out from a coiled stem. They grow on their own in swampy places and call for quite an effort while being picked. *Lingdaa* needs to be washed very well as it may carry soil and bacteria from the swamp. Like *poi*, this is a mucilaginous plant that is rich in nutrients. It carries high amounts of calcium, potassium, and iron. It is also rich in flavonoids, which are known to help in the prevention of certain cancers, as also cardiovascular and neuro degeneration. Like the *poi saag*, the slimy mucilage of *lingdaa* soothes the intestinal tract, facilitating smooth passage of food.

The taste of *lingdaa* is different, somewhat like a mix of young spinach and mushroom with a slight nutty flavour. The woman selling the saag told me to cook it using finely grated and chopped ginger, onions, and green chillies - a simple enough recipe. I later discovered that people go foraging for it even in some parts of Canada, where they add it to pastas and baked vegetables. It has the funny name of fiddlehead fern in English.

Fiddlehead greens (lingdaa), finely chopped
   **1 bunch, about 200 gm**

❀ Take
Oil in a pan **1 tsp/ 5ml**

❀ Place the greens in the pan.
❀ Add
Green chilli **1**

❀ After 2-3 minutes, add
Finely chopped onion **1 tsp/ 4 gm**
Finely grated ginger **1 tsp/ 5 gm** .
Salt **to taste**

❀ After a few minutes, the saag will be well cooked and ready to serve.

Washed fiddlehead ferns
Image Source:
Themightyquill/ Wikimedia Commons / CC BY-SA 3.0

# Ever Useful Coconut

*C*oconut is not indigenous to Rishikesh, but little shops abound with whole coconuts complete with their fibrous husks that make them stand up like skulls wearing peaked caps. The husked inner shell with its peculiar indentations does indeed look like a skull, complete with holes for the eyes and nose!

The reason for the abundance of coconut in Rishikesh may be because it makes for an important offering in ritual prayers in temples and sacred spaces. The structure of the 'nut' is symbolic of the structure of our universe. The fibrous husk represents the rough multi-skewered world that is not always the most hospitable. Beyond the husk is the woody covering that protects the inmost soft flesh and sweet liquid. The flesh is one singular mass, unlike the multifarious strands of the husk and stands on its own, pure and disconnected from the outer coverings.

The dehusking and cracking open of the nut calls for effort and skill. Once that is

Image Source: Ksenia Ilinykh / unsplash

Image Source: Irene Kredenets / unsplash

perfected, one can get to taste the sweet core. I always marvel at the graceful felicity with which the skilled ones crack the shell in one stroke, dividing it in two equal halves. The halves are offered to the gods, with the white core facing upward.

It shows that if we can pierce through the outer roughness and crack open the covering shell, we would get to the core untainted by external factors. It is that pure core that is offered to the Divine. Chunks of the white flesh are given out as prasad after prayers.

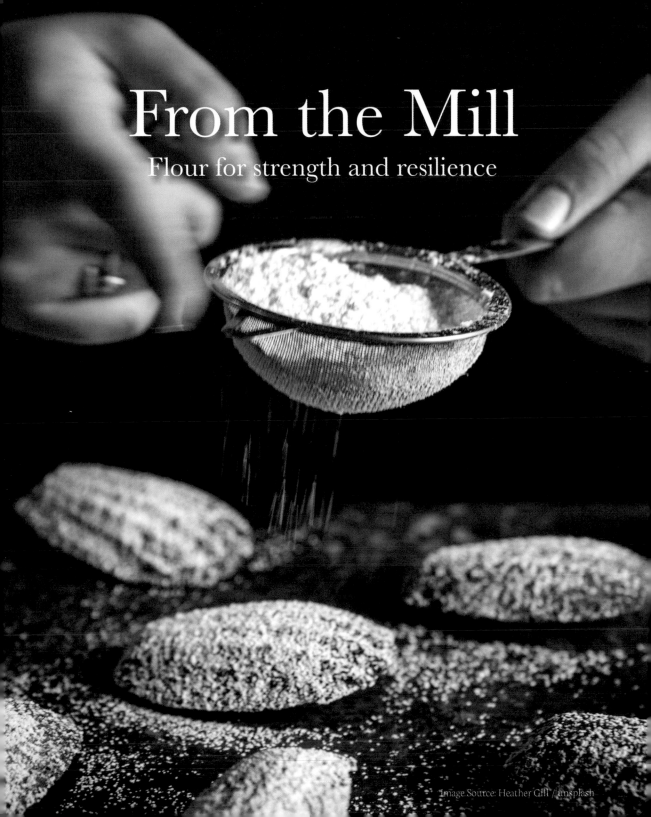

# From the Mill

## Flour for strength and resilience

A number of cereals and grains available at different times of the year in consonance with changing seasons act as alternates to the usual rice and wheat, and have traditionally been consumed extensively in this area. Among these grains is a large variety of millets, one of the oldest foods known to humans. Of these, *bajra* (pearl millet), *jowar* (sorghum), *ragi* (finger millet), *jhangora* (barnyard millet), *kodra* or *mandua* (kodo millet) are commonly available in markets all over India. Remarkable for their nutritive value, millets are known to be nearly 3–5 times nutritionally superior to rice and wheat, be it in their mineral content, vitamins, dietary fibre, or other nutrients. Being non-glutinous and non-acid forming, they are easily digestible. Most of them form a rich source of iron, calcium, zinc, magnesium, phosphorous, and potassium. Besides, the high dietary fibre content of millets goes into preventing constipation as well as some forms of cancer. This quality also makes them an important part of weight loss diets. This might have been the reason for the traditionally slender and sturdy physiques of hill people. *Jowar* (sorghum) is an important source of antioxidants and cholesterol-lowering elements. *Ragi* is rich in calcium, and *bajra* in iron. High amounts of vitamins of the B family and *lecithin* (please note the distinction between *lectin* in legumes and *lecithin* in millets) found in them are useful for strengthening the nervous system. Lecithin is a fatty substance that is essential for the cells of the body. It is good for preventing memory disorders such as dementia and Alzheimer's, as it is supposed to improve the brain's functional pathways. Among some well-known benefits of lecithin are its ability to raise HDL (good) cholesterol and lower LDL (bad) cholesterol, thus lowering the risk of hypertension. Its emulsifying qualities contribute to improving mucous in the intestine, helping to protect the delicate lining of the digestive system. These cereals, if consumed regularly, can make an important contribution to lowering the risk of nutritional deficiency.

Often labelled as 'coarse grains', consumption of millets has remained confined to traditional consumers, mainly in rural areas, perhaps because the processes involved in making them consumer-friendly are time-consuming and labour-intensive. Traditional methods of popping and flaking of various millets go into the making of ready-to-eat products that can be carried as one travels from one place to another. Many varieties, after being ground, can be fermented quite easily to make dishes like the delectable dosa or pancake.

Like legumes, millets also contribute to the environment. They help in reducing the atmospheric $CO_2$, thereby contributing to the maintenance of a healthy climate. Compared to this, paddy is known to emit methane and greenhouse gases ($CO^2$) from the water-drenched fields.

Flour from the mill

Besides, millet production does not require chemical fertilizers or pesticides, as the crops do not attract pests easily. Millets can grow in poor soil conditions and adapt to different climates. That is perhaps why so many varieties are found in different parts of India. They are a seasonal crop and are easily available from about October until March–April in this area. Due to their short growing season, they fit well into multiple cropping systems. Some varieties can even be seen planted on the boundaries of paddy fields.

Various millets blend well with other flours when making rotis, parathas, or even puris. They can also be used in baked products like biscuits, cookies, breads, cakes, muffins, etc.

Other than millets, there are crops like different varieties of soya, amaranth, water chestnut, chickpea, *sama* rice, *jhangora*, and others that provide wholesome and sustaining alternatives to rice and wheat flours. We tried many of these with considerable success so far as presentability and taste were concerned.

# BAKED SAVOURIES (CRACKERS) WITH SORGHUM AND DRY FENUGREEK

### Jowar aur kasoori methi ki mathri

PREPARATION TIME: 15–20 MINUTES | COOKING TIME: 20 MINUTES | 12–14 SERVINGS

Jowar, another fibre-rich (gluten-free) cereal is coming into the limelight due to the many nutrients it has. High in protein and iron, it is also packed with minerals and micronutrients. Its magnesium content helps healthy bones. When paired with a good vitamin C supplement, the iron in it is absorbed more easily. *Mathris* are usually made with white flour (maida) and are deep-fried. As such, they tend to become a little heavy on the digestive system. Here, other than using flours that are wholesome and protein-rich, the *mathris* were baked instead of being fried. The use of flax and chia seeds, as binding agents, further adds to the nutritional potential of these *mathris*.

Flax (*alsi*) seeds **1 tbsp/ 10 gm**
Chia seeds **1 tbsp/ 10 gm**
Black peppercorns, coarsely cracked **1 tsp/ 2 gm**

❁ Coarsely grind the flax and chia seeds in a blender and soak in
Water **6 tbsp**

❁ Set aside.

❁ Prepare the dough with the following ingredients in a big bowl or large plate
Sorghum flour (jowar atta) **½ cup/ 50 gm**
Chickpea or gram flour (besan) **½ cup/ 50 gm**
Semolina (sooji) **½ cup/ 60 gm**
Wheat flour (atta) **½ cup/ 60 gm**
Himalayan rock salt **1 tsp/ 4 gm**
Bishop's weed or carom (ajwain) **1 tsp/ 2 gm**

Dried fenugreek leaves (kasoori methi)
   **4 tbsp/ 8 gm**
White sesame seeds  **2 tsp/ 14 gm**
Red chilli powder  **¼ tsp, or a pinch**

⊛  Add the soaked flax/ chia blend into the
   mixture. Use your hands to fold the mixture
   evenly through the dough. Add
Peanut oil  **4 tbsp/ 40 ml**

⊛  Add it slowly into the mixture to bring the
   dough together. Knead it lightly till you get a
   nice doughy ball. (Sprinkle some water if the

dough is too dry.) Preheat oven to 200°C.
⊛  Divide the dough into 1" diameter balls.
   Flatten the balls using your palms and
   fingers into about 2" round discs or mathris.
   Press 2-3 pieces of cracked peppercorn into
   the centre.
⊛  Place on a baking sheet in the oven for 15-20
   minutes. Being dairy-free, the mathris last
   long in an airtight jar.

Other than being served as a snack these can
also serve as a side dish with a soup.

# OATMEAL AND FINGER MILLET COOKIES

## Mandua (finger millet), jowar (sorghum), aur bajre (pearl millet) ke biskut

PREPARATION TIME: 15–20 MINUTES | COOKING TIME: 20 MINUTES | MAKES 4 DOZEN

Cookies are a popular food in any cuisine. I remember, in my childhood when we lived in Shimla, fresh ingredients like good wholesome flour, pure ghee, and sugar were sent to a bakery to be turned into crisp biscuits that were always available in a jar at home. They made for a good, healthy snack in between meals. Now, in Rishikesh, we carried out a trial recipe with a combination of flours from several ancient grains, and it proved to be a success. A combination of flours helps derive nutrients from all of them. To bind them, we used a mixture of ground flax and chia seeds instead of eggs.

Rolled oats **1 cup/ 85 gm**
Ground flax seeds **½ cup/ 70 gm**
Finger millet (mandua flour) **½ cup/ 50 gm**
Sorghum (jowar) flour **½ cup/ 50 gm**
Pearl millet (bajra) flour **½ cup/ 50 gm**
Wheat flour (atta) **½ cup/ 60 gm**
Soy flour (soya atta) **½ cup/ 50 gm**
Organic brown sugar (bhoori shakkar)
  **½ cup/ 90 gm**
Chemical-free jaggery (gud) **½ cup/ 90 gm**
Coarsely ground chia and flax seeds mixed with
  water **6 tbsp**
  (chia beej aur alasi ka beej) **1 tbsp / 10 gm each**
  (this mix works as an egg substitute)
Baking powder **1 tsp/ 4 gm**
Baking soda **1 tsp/ 4 gm**
Cinnamon **1 tsp/ 3 gm**
Raisins **2 tbsp/ 20 gm**
Peanut oil **5 oz/ 120 gm**
Water **2 oz/ 50 ml**
Salt **a pinch as taste enhancer**

❀ Mix all the dry ingredients. Roll in raisins. Add the liquid flax seed mixture and then the oil. Add water to turn it into a thick consistency that will hold its shape when spooned out onto a baking sheet. Ladle out about 1½" diameter globules on to the baking dish. Keep some distance as they may spread slightly.

⊛ Bake in a slow oven (190°C) for 15 minutes on the middle rack. Then for 5 minutes on the lower rack. Test the cookies as they may take shorter or longer time depending on the consistency of the mixture. I got four batches of 12 cookies each (4 dozen in all).

⊛ Different flavours were put into the four parts. One had some red chilli powder, another a dash of lemon zest, the third one some dry grated coconut, and pumpkin seeds went into the last. An innovative and experimental baking produced four types of cookies.

They make a good in-between meal snack that is sustaining and nourishing. As they are dairy-free, the cookies last well in an airtight box and have a shelf life of at least 3–4 weeks.

# FINGER MILLET AND WHEAT FLOUR HALWA
## Mandua aur atte ka halwa

PREPARATION TIME: 20 MINUTES | COOKING TIME: 20–25 MINUTES | 8–10 SERVINGS

Halwa is another ubiquitous dish; any festival, any celebration tends to bring up some version of halwa. It forms an important offering to the gods of the Hindu pantheon. One of the attractions of the Sikh gurudwaras is the lovingly prepared rich halwa that is served as prasad. Halwas come in different varieties the world over. Here, we experimented with the local *mandua* flour, which has many nutrients and no gluten. We also added to it the usual atta and *sooji* (semolina).

❀ The following quantities may be halved if desired. The halwa freezes well and can be re-heated as and when needed. Dry roast separately.

Finger millet (mandua) flour  **1 cup/ 100 gm**
Wheat flour (atta)  **1 cup/ 110 gm**
Semolina (sooji)  **¾ cup/ 110 gm**

❀ These are to be roasted without any ghee or oil. Each one takes a different length of time till it is lightly browned and begins to exude a sweet smell.

❀ Now boil

Tagar, coarse sugar (boora), normal or crystallized sugar (mishri) may be used instead  **1 cup/ 140 gm**
Water  **4 cups/ about 850 ml**

❀ Add

Crushed cardamoms  **3-4**

❀ Set aside the mix. Now heat

Ghee  **1 cup/ 220 ml**

❀ Add the roasted flours and fry till the ghee begins to separate from the flours.

❀ Add

Raisins  **2 tbsp/ 20 gm**
Pumpkin seeds  **2 tbsp/ 20 gm**
Cuddapah almond (chironji)  **1 tbsp/10 gm**

❀ Slowly pour the hot coarse sugar (boora) water and stir. Cook till the water is absorbed and the halwa gains a semi-dry consistency and leaves the sides of the pan. Serve warm.

✺ Apart from dessert, halwa is also served with puris.

# FINGER MILLET KADHI
## Mandua ki kadhi

PREPARATION TIME: 5 MINUTES | COOKING TIME: 20-25 MINUTES | 2 SERVINGS

The versatility of *mandua*, or finger millet, emboldens one's exploratory tendency. So taking cues from local uses, I felt motivated to try some hybrids. The cereal, also called ragi in many parts of India (as it has many varieties), is said to have been grown in India for some 4,000 years and is known to contain more proteins and minerals than other cereals and millets. Traditionally, a staple with the hill people of Uttarakhand, it kept them healthy and strong. *Kadhi* is a general favourite in North India and goes well with both rice and roti. A *kadhi* made from *mandua* is both light and flavourful. Another attractive part is the ease of preparation.

Finger millet (mandua) flour **¼ cup/ 25 gm**
Yoghurt **½ cup/ 100gm/ 100ml**
Water to make a thin mixture

Wild mustard (jakhiya) **⅓ tsp/1 gm**
Mustard seeds **½ tsp/1 gm**
Fenugreek seeds **½ tsp/2 gm**

❀ Beat the yoghurt in a bowl. Add water and the finger millet (mandua) flour to make a thin mixture, the consistency of rich, full cream milk. Add

Turmeric (haldi) **½ tsp/ 1gm**
Cumin (jeera) powder **½ tsp/ 1 gm**
Coriander (dhania) powder **½ tsp/ 1 gm**
Dry ginger powder (saunth) **½ tsp/ 1 gm**
Himalayan rock salt **1 tsp/ 4 gm**

❀ Cook on slow fire, stirring, to avoid any lumps. Cook till the mixture gains a thick (rabri or custard-like) consistency, and the mandua is cooked. Turn off heat.
❀ In a small pan, heat
Ghee **1 tbsp/10 ml**
Curry leaves **a few**

❀ Let splutter and pour over the kadhi. It is ready to be served when cooled for a few minutes. More ghee may be added when serving, as per preference.

✤ Kadhi with rice is a favourite of many.

# FENUGREEK AND PEARL MILLET KADHI
## Methi aur bajre ki kadhi

PREPARATION TIME: 10 MINUTES | COOKING TIME: 20–25 MINUTES | 2 SERVINGS

Methi blends well with many food items. We also used it for a kadhi, which we prepared with *bajra* flour instead of the usual chickpea flour. The bitter, pungent methi leaves appear in the winter season. Packed with antioxidants, they are known to help in weight loss as the fibre in them gives a feeling of satiety, thus preventing a sense of craving for more food. Fibre also helps the movement of food through the intestines, thus helping to promote better metabolism. The micronutrient-rich *bajra* or pearl millet, which has been grown in India since millennia, is also a popular grain during winter. Methi leaves and *bajra* blend well to make a satisfying dish.

❀ Keep aside
Fenugreek (methi) leaves, chopped **1 cup/ 75 gm**

❀ Mix the following ingredients in a bowl before placing on the stove.
Yogurt **1 cup/ 200 gm/ 200 ml**
Water **2 cups/ 400 ml**
Pearl millet (bajra) flour **½ cup/ 50 gm**

❀ Mix yogurt with water till smooth. Mix in the millet (bajra) flour and beat till smooth. Place over medium heat and add
Himalayan rock salt (saindha namak) **2 tsp/ 8 gm**
Coriander (dhania) powder **1 tsp/ 2 gm**
Cumin (jeera) powder **1 tsp/ 2 gm**
Turmeric (haldi) powder **½ tsp/ 1 gm**

❀ Keep stirring. Add the fenugreek leaves and cook for about 15 minutes till it thickens to the consistency of a buttermilk or lassi.

❀ In a separate pan, heat
Mustard oil **1 tbsp/10 ml**
Dry red chillies **2 whole**
Brown mustard seeds **1 tsp/ 3 gm** (let splutter)

❀ Now add
Freshly grated ginger **1 tbsp/10 gm**
Fresh curry leaves **8-12 whole**

❀ Cook for a few minutes till blended. Add the yogurt mixture and continue cooking. Then add
Powdered asafoetida (hing) **1 tsp/ 1 gm**
Grated chemical free jaggery (gud) **½ tbsp/ 8 gm**

❀ Cook for 5 more minutes and take off the stove. It is ready to be served when cooled.

# AMARANTH SEEDS AND BLACK GRAM FRITTERS
## Chaulai aur urad pakodi

PREPARATION TIME: 15 MINUTES | COOKING TIME: 10 MINUTES | 2 SERVINGS

As in other parts of India, in Uttarakhand also, people commonly make black gram (*urad*) daal *vada*, or *pakodi*. That is a well-known dish. Try out a preparation with amaranth; the seed is commonly available in the Himalayan foothills, and flour made from it is also used during periods of fasting. Certain dry preparations made from the popped seeds not only make for good fasting food, but provide nutrition that other snack foods would be lacking. The first time I saw amaranth was in its bright red flower form when trekking in the upper reaches of the Himalayas. The hillsides were ablaze with the crimson hue of this semi-cereal plant that has a short maturation period.

Amaranth leaves make for a tasty and nutritious saag, while the seeds are used whole or milled into flour. The small, gluten-free seeds are rich in proteins like quinoa. They are also rich in calcium, magnesium, potassium, phosphorus, and iron, and are a good source of vitamin C and iron.

❁ Soak in water (for 5-6 hours)
Amaranth seeds **½ cup/ 90 gm**

❁ In a separate container, soak
Black gram (urad) daal **¼ cup/ 40 gm**
(Use the de-husked white-coloured daal made
from black gram)
Fenugreek (methi) seeds **½ tsp/ 2 gm**
(may be added to the daal)

❁ Grind both separately to form
sticky pastes. Combine
the two and add
Himalayan rock salt **to taste**
Green chilli, finely chopped **1**
Fresh ginger, finely grated **½ " piece/ 5 gm**

Green coriander, finely chopped **1 tbsp/ 4 gm**
Arugula leaves (if available), finely chopped **a few**

❀ Let the mixture stand for 2-3 hours.
Then steam the mixture for 10-12 minutes
by placing the pan containing the
mixture in a larger pan, putting a
little water in the larger pan, and letting the
water simmer.

❀ Then put tablespoonfuls of this steamed
batter onto a ¼" layer of oil heated in a
skillet. The pakodis can be made smaller
by putting teaspoonfuls of the mixture
instead of a larger quantity. These

delicious and nutritious pakodis do not
soak in too much oil when cooking. They
can be accompanied with a chutney of
choice.

❀ One could also try to make them without
steaming the mixture, but it does not turn
out so good and also soaks in too much oil.

Serve with a favoured chutney (p. 117).

# Roti and Chilla

Unleavened flat breads cooked in various ways are a staple in Indian cuisine. The breads can be varied as they can be made from many different flours, and/ or with several other ingredients. This gives them a character of their own, and enables their consumption even without an accompanying vegetable or daal, as they can be taken as a snack with tea or as a breakfast dish.

Freshly made or even heated up frozen rotis provide a sense of satiation and a feeling of wholesomeness. The variety of attas that are available in this area of the Himalayan foothills around Rishikesh allow for different kinds of rotis to be made at different times of the year and to suit different tastes.

Cornflour (*makki*) and pearl millet (*bajra*) rotis are popular in the winter and they pair well with a variety of saags – the leafy greens – that are available at that time of the year. Rotis can also be prepared from non-cereal flours like water-chestnut (*singhara*) flour, buckwheat (*kuttu*) flour, and amaranth flour (*ramdana*), especially during times of fasting. These are lighter and very easy to digest.

Here we give a couple of suggestions, which can act as a take-off point for experimentation with different flours, using different leaves and stuffings.

# SWEET PEARL MILLET BREAD
## Bajre ki meethi roti

*Bajra* (pearl millet) is commonly available in the winter. Like *mandua*, this also is rich in protein, fibre, phosphorous, magnesium, and iron. The gluten-free cereal is easy to digest. Often thick, hand-patted rotis are prepared and consumed with a dollop of ghee. A sweeter version of it can be had with any savoury daal or vegetable preparation.

Pearl millet (bajre) ka atta  **3 cups/ 300 gm**

❀ Add to it
Fennel (moti saunf)  **1 tbsp/ 5 gm**
Himalayan rock salt (saindha namak)
  **1 tsp/ 4 gm**
Salt  **a pinch**

❀ Heat
Grated jaggery (gud)  **1 cup/ 180 gm**
Water **½ cup**
Ghee  **2-3 tbsp/ 20-30 ml**

❀ Pour the jaggery and melted ghee into the dry ingredients and mix into a pliable dough.

❀ Divide the dough into balls (the size of golf balls – this may make six rotis) and flatten them using your hands. The roti may be about ¼" thick or a little more.

❀ Cook on a griddle (tawa) and flip when one side looks done. You may cover the roti when it is being cooked to ensure that the dough is cooked through. It will also give it a crisp texture.

❀ Apply a generous quantity of ghee on the rotis.

The rotis may be served with any well-seasoned daal or a green vegetable. The salty accompaniment to these sweet rotis makes for a delectable combination.

Note: Can be vegan without the ghee.

# COLOCASIA LEAF BREAD
## Arvi ke patte ki roti

PREPARATION TIME: 15–20 MINUTES | COOKING TIME: 20–25 MINUTES | 4 ROTIS

Colocasia (*arvi*), a variety of yam, is usually sown around June and harvested after Diwali in October or November. The leaves may be available for use in the rainy season. They are rich in antioxidants and beta carotenes. Vitamin A in them is good for eyesight and the skin. It also contains essential minerals like zinc, magnesium, and potassium. These help regulate heart rate and blood pressure.

When using colocasia (*arvi*) leaves make sure to use the new, fresh shoots and even those that grow below them as the mature leaves can cause an itchiness on the tongue and throat because they carry calcium oxalate crystals that keep them protected from bugs. If the leaf is a bit larger, then remove the veins-particularly the one central vein-and wash them very well. Cutting them very fine and cooking them long enough rids them of these itch-causing crystals.

Colocasia leaves are used in many ways in different parts of India. We prepared a delicious roti with it.

❀ To make the roti take
Arvi leaves, finely chopped **4/ approximately 2 cups**

❀ Add to the leaves
Finely chopped or grated ginger **2 tsp/ 10 gm**
Finely chopped green chillies **4**
Carom (ajwain) **½ tsp/ 1 gm**
Himalayan rock salt **1 tsp/ 4 gm**
Cold pressed mustard oil **2 tsp/10 ml**

❀ Mix all the ingredients well and slowly add
Gram flour (besan) **½ cup/ 50 gm**
Wheat flour (atta) **½ cup/ 60 gm**

❀ The flours – besan and atta – should be just enough to bind the leaves. The leaves should remain the main ingredient, and not the flours. When the dough reaches the right consistency for rolling out into rotis, prepare rotis as usual. In this case, just make sure to keep the heat low. Cover the roti when it is being cooked so that the leaves are cooked through. A little oil may be applied to it when the roti is flipped over to be cooked on the other side.

The rotis can be had with vegetables, or a dollop of butter or malai. They can be served for breakfast or a main meal. If there is some itching and irritation from the rough texture of the leaves, consumption of a little buttermilk or yoghurt will help.

# FINGER MILLET PANCAKES
## Mandua ka chilla

PREPARATION TIME: 5 MINUTES + 10 MINUTES RESTING TIME  |
COOKING TIME: 5–10 MINUTES  |  ABOUT 6 CHILLAS

*Mandua, koda,* or finger millet is a hardy, drought-tolerant annual crop that can survive on marginal soils. *Koda* millet has the potential to act as a nourishing food for subsistence farmers. *Mandua* roti or paratha, served with *gehat* (or *kulath*) daal, is a staple in Uttarakhand. Rich in protein and calcium, this gluten free flour is easy to digest and has a flavour unique to it. Its rich dark colour is an indication of the high iron content in this cereal grain, which also carries a number of vitamins of the B category, and a good amount of dietary fibre. The rotis are commonly made with just *mandua* flour, patted thick. They can also be mixed with wheat flour and rolled thin and cooked on a griddle.

We tried it out as a *chilla* (an Indian version of pancake, or a 'roti' prepared with a watery mix of flour and other ingredients). The flour took on a sort of fermented quality after it was mixed with water and left for a few minutes. *Chillas* are light and make for a healthy and nutritious breakfast food when served with a chutney of one's choice. Both green and coconut chutneys can be used as they enhance the flavour of the flour and add a zest to the dish.

In North India, a well-known popular version of this is made by using just *besan* (chickpea) flour, instead of any of the aforementioned ingredients.

Finger millet (mandua) flour **1 cup/ 120 gm**
Bishop's weed, carom (ajwain) **½ tsp/ 1 gm**
Salt **to taste**
Freshly chopped coriander (dhania)
  **4 tbsp/ 15 gm**
Finely chopped green chilli **1**
Finely chopped garlic **½ tsp/ 2 gm**
Finely grated ginger **1 tsp/ 5 gm**
Water **1 cup/ 220 ml** (enough to bring it to a
  dosa or pancake-like consistency.

❀ Mix all the ingredients well and let the batter rest for 10 minutes. Ladle the batter onto a non-stick pan and spread it out to the size of a roti, or any desired size.
❀ Add a few drops of oil around the chilla and allow to cook till lightly brown on one side. Then flip and cook the other side. Your chilla is ready!

❀ A very successful alternate version was tried out in my kitchen, using
Pearl millet (bajra) flour **½ cup/ 50 gm**
Makki (corn) flour **½ cup/ 50 gm**
Soy flour **½ cup/ 50 gm**
Finger millet (mandua) flour **½ cup/ 60 gm**

❀ Then add
Finely chopped onion **2 tbsp/ 8 gm**
Finely grated ginger **1 tbsp/ 10 gm**
Finely chopped green chillies **2**
Finely chopped coriander
(or any other green that
may be available) **a handful**
Salt **to taste**

❀ Add water to make it a pancake-batter consistency. Leave aside for about 20 minutes.

✎ The dosa (pancake) made from this mixture is especially delicious, as it has a nutty flavour and can be served with anything - yoghurt, butter, pickles, or chutney. It may be served for breakfast or for any other meal. Being gluten-free, it is easy to digest. The high fibre content helps the gastric processes.

Note: Chillas may be prepared in advance and lightly heated on a griddle before serving.

# AMARANTH SEED PANCAKE
## Ramdana ka chilla

PREPARATION TIME: 15 MINUTES + 15 MINUTES REST |
COOKING TIME: 10 MINUTES  |  MAKES 4 PIECES

*Ramdana* (amaranth), a pseudo cereal, is also called *rajgira*, the king of cereals, because of the extraordinary nutritional value it has. Even the English word 'amaranth' refers to its undying quality, as it is a perennial plant and is also regarded as a life-enhancer, a super health food. Though seen (and cooked) as a gluten-free cereal or grain, it is actually not a grain but a seed. Since it is not a grain, it is extensively used as a food during ritualistic fasting. Its leaves make for an enriching and tasty leafy green, or saag. Another leafy vegetable, *bathua* (*Chenopodium album*, also called goosefoot, lamb's quarters, or pigweed in the USA; a very popular leafy green in northern India and consumed mostly in winter, often mixed in the delicious and nutritious Punjabi preparation *sarson da saag*) also belongs to the same family. Amaranth has more protein than quinoa and much more than other grains like wheat or rice. Besides, the quality of protein obtained from these two grains is far superior to other commonly used grains. Amaranth provides twice the amount of iron as compared to quinoa. It also provides a larger proportion of vitamins of the B group as compared to quinoa. This seed or 'grain' is easy to cook and lends itself to a variety of uses in the kitchen. Here, we used it for making *chillas*/ savoury pancakes that can be had either for breakfast or as cereals during a main meal.

Rajgira **½ cup / 100 gm**
Water, as needed
Onion, finely chopped  **1 tbsp / 10 gm**
Green chilli, finely chopped **½ tsp / 2 gm**
Fresh ginger, finely chopped  **1 tsp / 5 gm**
Coriander, or dardmar, or any green leaves  **1 tbsp / 7 gm**
Salt, as per taste
Cooking oil  **1 tbsp / 10 gm**

✵ Grind the rajgir to powder in a coffee grinder. It may be reduced to very fine granules. Add the finely chopped herbs and water till it gains a pancake-like pouring consistency. Let the mix sit for about 15 minutes and then with a ladle pour small scoops on to a heated frying pan, which has a little oil on it. Let cook on one side and then flip to cook the other side. (The batter may tend to spread out. It may be a good idea to pour a dollop and then let it spread.)

It may be served with any preferred chutney or with cooked vegetables.

# AMARANTH SEED PIZZA
## Ramdana ka pizza

PREPARATION TIME: 25–30 MINUTES + 2-3 HOURS SOAKING |
COOKING TIME: 20 MINUTES | 4 SERVINGS

This Himalayan gluten-free pizza is light and easy on the system, even as it carries the goodness of amaranth seeds (*ramdana*). It is easy to make and can be stored in the fridge for a few days.

**For the base**
Ramdana ²/₃ cup / 125 gm
Water ²/₃ cup / 150 ml
Chia **1 tsp/4 gm** soaked in 2 tsp water for 10
  minutes
Parmesan cheese, finely grated **5 tbsp / 25 gm**

Salt **to taste**
Black pepper **¼ tsp / 2 gm**
Oregano **½ tsp / 4 gm**

**Topping**
Onion, thinly sliced **½ of one**

Garlic, finely chopped **¼ tsp/ 2 gm**
Himalayan spinach (pahadi palak) finely chopped
   **1 bunch/75 gm**
Water chestnut (singhara), shelled and sliced
   **5-6 pieces/ 50 gm**

❀ Canned water chestnuts may be used.
Olive oil **1 tsp / 5 gm**
Himalayan cucumber (pahadi kheera) thinly
   sliced **1 small**
Red and yellow peppers **few slices**
Tomato, sliced into wedges **1**
Mozzarella cheese **50 gm**
Olive oil **½ tsp / 2 gm**

❀ To prepare the dough, wash the ramdana
and run the water out through a fine sieve
to remove any dust or grit. Boil the ramdana
in water, till soft and cooked. It may be
pre-soaked for 2-3 hours for easy cooking.
The water will dry up in the cooking. More
water may be used in case the ramdana is
not soft. Add seasoning. Stir in the soaked
chia . Turn off fire and blend in parmesan
cheese. On a greased, flat baking tray, pour
out the mixture and spread it into an 8"

(approximately) round. Let set for
a few minutes.

❀ Turn on the oven to 200°C.

❀ For the topping, pour one teaspoon of olive
oil in a skillet. Add sliced onions. Cook for a
minute or two till softened, add garlic and
then pahadi palak. Cook for 2-3 minutes and
then add the sliced water chestnuts. Cook for
another 2-3 minutes. Add salt and pepper.

❀ (Water chestnuts can be sliced easily by
cutting the 'nut' lengthwise to expose the
heart-shaped white kernel inside. The outer
shell can then be removed with ease.) Smear
the cucumber and pepper slices and tomatoes
with ½ tsp olive oil and keep aside. Spread the
cooked vegetable mixture on the pizza base
and top with cucumber and pepper slices and
tomatoes. Place slices of mozzarella on the
topping. Place in the oven and let cook for
20-25 minutes.

❀ It is possible that the base spreads a little. That
is alright. If lifting out the whole pizza proves
to be a little difficult due to the soft base, cut it
into slices and take them out.

🌿 The pizza may be served with a green salad.

# Vegan Delights

For the animals, for the planet, for our health

Leguminous milk

Rishikesh draws all kinds of people into its vortex. Two of them who ambled into our cookbook are David and Lakshman. David, from Denmark, gave up his lucrative job he got after finishing studies at the London School of Economics and came here to pursue yoga, explore health foods, and follow a vegan diet. He is much dedicated to permaculture and working in gardens. His friend Lakshman gave up his architectural training, which he completed in Denmark, and travelled to Rishikesh. A vegan, he volunteered in an organic café at Rishikesh for some time. He and David decided to show us how to make 'paneer' from chickpea flour, and yoghurt from red rice and peanuts for those who do not wish to consume dairy.

Vegans can be called *shuddh shakahaari* in Hindi; they are strict vegetarians who do not consume even dairy products. So milk, paneer, dahi, cream, kheer, milk custard, butter, or cheese are not vegan food. I substituted black *bhatt* and soyabeans for rice to cut down on carbohydrates and starch. Those who do not like peanuts may use a combination of red or brown rice and soyabeans. All the preparations made from the vegan paneer, as also from the 'leguminous milk', came out to be delectable even for the non-vegans. I also prepared a raita and a version of *crème brûlée* using the 'leguminous milk'. Both are easily digestible and light on the system.

Though most dishes in this book can be consumed by vegans, we provide here some particular dishes that vegans may enjoy and share with their non-vegan friends.

# VEGAN PANEER

Gram flour (*besan*), made by grinding a certain type of chana daal (one type of Bengal gram) is a versatile flour that is used for preparing both sweet and savoury dishes. Its texture, flavour, nutritional value, and adaptability make it a good substitute for some dairy products such as paneer. It is gluten-free and has a higher content of carbohydrates and protein as compared to other flours.

❈ Mix together

Chickpea flour (besan) **1½ cup/ 150 gm**

Water **2 cups/ 400 ml**

❈ Stir it well so that it gains a smooth, pancake-like or even thicker custard-like consistency. When the mixture is free of all lumps, add

Salt **to taste**

Ground cumin **½ tsp/ 1 gm**

Ground coriander **½ tsp/ 1 gm**

Ground fenugreek seeds **½ tsp/ 1 gm**

Finely chopped, green chilli **1**

Finely chopped, green coriander **1 tbsp/ 4 gm**
  (or more, if liked)

❈ Chopped arugula (rocket) leaves may be added for a different flavour.

❈ Place it on the stove, stirring constantly. Very soon, within a few minutes, it gains a thick pasty consistency. Pat the pasty mixture onto a flat-bottomed dish large enough to allow a thickness of about ¾" or more, and press some oregano and basil flakes on it. After the paste cools down (it can be placed in fridge to cool, if needed), cut it into squares.

❈ Lightly pan-fry the pieces to a toasty texture in a non-stick pan with barely a touch of oil. Coconut oil adds a nice flavour to the flour. Then garnish with toasted sesame seeds to be served with a chutney, or dip of choice.

The 'paneer' cubes can be cooked for a few minutes in a gravy of choice and served as a main dish to go with rice, rotis, or parathas. Or with a dish of green peas and tomatoes.

# VEGAN RAITA

PREPARATION TIME: 15–20 MINUTES + SOAKING TIME |
COOKING TIME: 5 MINUTES + TIME FOR SETTING

First, the vegan 'leguminous milk' needs to be prepared before it can be turned into yoghurt or other preparations. We substituted the brown rice, suggested by our vegan friends, with black *bhatt* (local soya). For a strict vegan, one would need to buy a commercial vegan yoghurt for the first culture. Not following such strict norms the first time, we used a teaspoon of regular yoghurt culture. Subsequent cultures came from the yoghurt that was prepared from this mixture. Some of the culture can also be frozen till such time as needed, since it freezes well. The process is simple. The milk, once made, can be stored in the fridge for a few days and used for different preparations.

- For the leguminous milk, soak separately for 7-8 hours

Raw peanuts (preferably the organic variety)
   ½ cup/ 60 gm
Himalayan soyabean (black bhatt)
   ¼ cup/ 40 gm

- The legumes might even begin to show signs of sprouting. That is quite okay. The soaking and sprouting processes help to get rid of much of the lectins that the two may carry. The remaining amount can be comfortably absorbed by most people. Some amounts of lectins are even good, as they fight some harmful microbes and aid the processes of absorption in the large intestines.
- Grind the two legumes separately till there are almost no granules remaining. Add more water if needed. Some granules may add to the texture by making it a little crunchy.
- Combine the two and add water to get a thick creamy-milk like consistency. Boil the mixture for 4-5 minutes, stirring all the time, to prevent it sticking to the bottom of the pan.
- Cool a little.
- For the raita, take some of the mixture in a bowl, while still more than luke warm. Add a teaspoonful of the regular culture and mix well. You may use a wire whisk to give it a good beating. Cover and leave it in a warm place for 6-7 hours to set. The yoghurt is ready. Place in the fridge to cool. Now the required amount can be taken and turned into a delectable raita. This is done by adding the preferred ingredient into the yoghurt.
- Just add some black salt, a touch of organic brown sugar (bhoori shakkar), a little red chilli, roasted cumin powder, and some finely chopped green coriander.
- Other versions can be made with grated cucumber or just raisins, along with the spices preferred.

Yoghurt can be taken as needed along with rotis or rice.

# VEGAN BRÛLÉE

PREPARATION TIME: 5 MINUTES  |  COOKING TIME: 5 MINUTES  |  4 SERVINGS

This is a take-off from a soya milk recipe prepared by my young Japanese friend Michiko, who runs a homestyle Japanese restaurant here. The light texture, delicate flavour, and the easy-on-the-system dish proves to be quite a favourite with most people.

In this recipe, the soya milk has been substituted by 'leguminous milk', which may be a little more flavourful. Even though this may call for a little more preparation, it would be favourable for those who cannot take soya. The 'leguminous milk' may be prepared in advance and stored in the fridge for three or four days, or more. The *brûlée* can also be stored in the fridge for a few days.

❀ Heat
Leguminous milk  **2 cups/ 400 ml**
❀ Add to the milk
Cornflour (also known as cornstarch)  **3 tsp/ 6 gm**
mixed to a smooth paste in  **a little water**
Organic brown sugar (bhoori shakkar)  **2 tbsp/ 16 gm**

❀ Bring to boil and stir for 2-3 minutes.

❀ Take it off the fire and stir for a few more minutes to prevent a film from forming on top.
❀ Pour the mixture into small serving bowls and let sit in the fridge.

Serve with honey, or a syrup made from jaggery (gud) boiled with some water, or with maple syrup.

# PUMPKIN PANCAKES

PREPARATION TIME: 20–25 MINUTES + SOAK TIME FOR PEANUTS |
COOKING TIME: 10 MINUTES | MAKES 8–10 PANCAKES

This makes for a light dessert-like dish, which can be had at any time as a snack also. The minimal amounts of *mandua* and wheat flour make it almost gluten-free. The flax and chia seeds used for binding add to the nutrients of the pumpkin and peanuts. Both flax and chia serve as egg substitutes, and both are high in omega-3 fatty acids. They improve heart health, and may help in conditions such as rheumatism and prevent Alzheimer's. Flax seeds provide a nutty flavour to the dish, while the chia just remain a gelatinous non-flavour substance.

❀ Scrape the skin of the pumpkin well and let some tender part of it remain. Steam the pumpkin and blend to make it into a puree.

❀ Mix

Pumpkin puree **2 cups/ 250 gm**

Peanuts soaked for 2-3 hours and then ground in a blender **½ cup/ 60 gm**

❀ Add

Finger millet (mandua) flour **2 tbsp/ 16 gm**

Wheat flour (atta) **3 tbsp/ 24 gm**

❀ Grind together coarsely and add

Cloves **4-5**

Cardamoms **5-6**

Nutmeg **small piece**

Cinnamon (or use powdered cinnamon) **small stick**

❀ Add

Baking powder **¼ tsp/ 1 gm, or less**

Baking soda **¼ tsp/ 1 gm**

Honey **2 tbsp/ 40 gm**

❀ Add to this a mixture of

Coarsely ground chia **1 tbsp/ 8 gm**

Coarsely ground flax **1 tbsp/ 10 gm**

❀ Soak both in 6 tbsp water and leave for a few minutes to form a gelatinous substance.

❀ Pour spoonfuls of the mixture onto a non-stick pan. Keep some distance as they may spread. Sprinkle some coconut oil, cover, and leave on low flame for 8-10 minutes. When one side is browned, flip and cook the other side. The pancakes will be slightly thick. If the mixture is too runny, add a little more flour.

Serve with syrup made from gud or with maple syrup.

Note: This recipe can be gluten free if wheat flour is replaced by another millet flour.

Both these seeds are superfoods, as they carry high amounts of calcium, phosphorous, and some vitamins of the B group. High in fibre, their gelatinous component provides good aid to the peristaltic function in the digestive system. *Chia* was first introduced to me by a friend's father in Mumbai. They called it *sabja*. Later, I realized that *sabja* is a little different from chia. Actually, it refers to the seeds of basil. Both belong to the mint family. *Flax* seeds, called *alsi*, are commonly available in grocery shops.

The two seeds have very similar qualities, though they differ somewhat in the amounts of certain nutrients. Chia seeds are supposed to have 25% more fibre and phosphorus and even double the amount of calcium found in flax seeds. Flax seeds, on their part, have larger amounts of the brain-boosting vitamin B1 as compared to chia. The small chia seeds can be consumed whole without losing their nutritional benefits, whereas it is better to grind flax seeds, even coarsely, to help release their nutrients. Flax seeds carry a nutty flavour, while chia remains neutral.

Both can serve as egg substitutes, hence are doubly beneficial for vegans. I use a blend of the two when substituting for eggs. One tablespoon of the coarse blend mixed with three tablespoons of water, left aside for 5-10 minutes, gives a gelatinous single-egg-like binding substance.

Other than this, I make a blend of the two coarsely ground seeds and add to it ground sesame, pumpkin seeds, hemp, and any other seed that I may find useful, and store in a jar in the fridge. A tablespoon or so of this mixture makes for a good breakfast booster.

# Raitas

For the yoghurt lovers

Raitas are a favoured addition to meals in Uttarakhand, and many parts of India. With yoghurt or curd as their base, they become a good source of calcium and protein. The addition of a vegetable or herb adds to the taste, as also the nutritional value. Their creamy texture and the sweet-sour taste turns a regular meal into a celebration.

Raitas make the food more digestible by introducing some much-needed enzymes into the system. Curd or yoghurt in its natural form, or as buttermilk or raita, has remained a favoured food for millennia. It contains friendly bacteria that help break down food, absorb nutrients, and also fight some unfriendly disease-causing microbes. The bacteria involved in the process of fermentation, when preparing curd, carry enzymes that turn most of the lactose into lactic acid, thus making the milk easier to digest. Enzymes produced by these bacteria also help degrade a variety of fats, oils, proteins, and starches to make them suitable for the body. These bacteria are the life-giving probiotics. Probiotics, meaning 'for life', are bacteria that pass through the system undigested till they reach the gut where they assist in absorption, and elimination of toxins and wastes. They, in turn, are fed by the soluble fibre called prebiotic found in legumes and vegetables. Some commercial yoghurts even add on extra probiotics into their culture. But most commercialized yogurts also contain added sugars, artificial ingredients, and fillers. Home-made yogurt, or curd, is a better way of obtaining probiotics without introducing unnecessary chemicals into the body.

In Rishikesh, I use the full-cream milk we get here, as the other choice is double-toned, which is a highly watered-down version of milk. After boiling the milk and cooling it, I remove the thick layer of cream (which goes into other preparations), thus getting a reasonably fat-removed, yet rich-textured version of milk. It makes for curd that has both body and a good taste.

Curd or yoghurt is used in many ways – for raitas, buttermilk, *kadhi*. It also makes a good addition to many recipes during the process of cooking. A popular raita in this area is made by adding grated cucumber together with some spices to beaten yoghurt. Considering there is a plethora of vitamin-rich greens in the area, we tried some of our own. Each raita carries its unique flavour and colour.

# LAMB'S QUARTERS OR PIGWEED GREENS IN YOGHURT
## Bathua raita

PREPARATION TIME: 15–20 MINUTES | 2 SERVINGS

As it grows naturally without any effort in between the winter crops of maize, wheat, jowar, etc. the humble pigweed or *bathua* has remained a somewhat neglected green even when it plays an important role in the upkeep of the body. Despite occasional use in parathas, or *rotis*, or as an addition to other saags, it remains a less respected leaf. The selenium, Omega 3 and 6 fatty acids in it make *bathua* a great preventive against stones, breast cancer, and joint pains. Fresh *bathua* leaves, heated on a griddle and applied to painful joints, are known to provide relief.

*Bathua* comes in red and green varieties. The red one is more nutritious, but the green leaf also is full of goodness. Both have a specific taste, which add flavour to any dish they are put into. To enjoy its flavour without interference from any other vegetable, we used it in a raita.

❀ Prepare

Pigweed (bathua) **1 small bunch/ 100 gm**

❀ Wash it well. With a minimum amount of water, bring to boil and cook for 2-3 minutes.

❀ Overcooking will deplete the colour. Lightly crush or coarsely chop the cooked bathua. Set aside and let it cool. Lightly beat

Yoghurt **1 cup/ 200 gm/ 200 ml**

❀ Add

Black salt (kala namak) **1 tsp/ 4 gm**

Ground roasted jeera **1 tsp/ 4 gm**

Red chilli powder **¼ tsp/ 1 gm**

Organic brown sugar (bhoori shakkar) **½ tsp/ 2 gm**

❀ Add the cooled, crushed bathua. A little water or milk may be added if the yoghurt is too thick. It may be better to add this after putting in the bathua, as that may also make it more liquidy. Sprinkle the dish with some powdered roasted jeera and red chilli powder as a garnish.

❀ Bathua can be substituted by spinach if liked. The spinach should be cut into fine long strands and lightly steamed for 2-3 minutes. Allow it to cool and add to the yoghurt in the same way.

All raitas can be served as a side dish to accompany rotis, parathas or chillas.

# DRIED DATES AND FENNEL GREENS YOGHURT
## Chhuare aur saunf ka raita

PREPARATION TIME: 10 MINUTES + SOAK TIME  |  2 SERVINGS

We used dried dates, *chhuara*, in many ways both for its delectable flavour and the goodness of minerals with which it is saturated. *Chhuara* is an important source of iron, calcium, potassium, magnesium, phosphorus, copper, and selenium, and has been known for its constipation-relieving qualities. It can be seen as a kind of mineral-rich superfood. When combined with some other flavours like fenugreek, ginger, or fennel, the rich taste of the date is enhanced manifold.

For this raita, we added some delicate saunf, or fennel sprigs to the raita. The fennel was taken from our little garden where, once planted, it bloomed abundantly. If fennel sprigs cannot be found, then fresh coriander or pudina may be used. Even though these two herbs have their own strong flavours, they still blend well with the *chhuara*.

❀ For the raita
Dried dates (chhuaras) **4**

❀ Soak in water for 3-4 hours, then
   slice into thin slivers
Fresh fennel leaves, washed well, and
   chopped fine **2 sprigs**

❀ Then prepare
Yoghurt **1 cup/ 200ml/ 200 gm**

❀ Lightly beat it along with
Black salt (kala namak) **1 tsp/ 4 gm**
Ground roasted cumin (jeera) **1 tsp/ 2 gm**
Powdered red chilli **½ tsp/ 1 gm**

❀ Add the slivered dates and chopped fennel
   sprigs. Some more fennel leaves can be placed

on the yoghurt along with a little chilli powder and ground jeera as a garnish.

# BOTTLE GOURD IN TANGY YOGHURT
## Lauki ka raita

PREPARATION TIME: 10 MINUTES | 2–4 SERVINGS

Bottle gourd, or *lauki*, is another versatile vegetable that can be used in many different ways. It lends itself to roasting, to cooking as a vegetable, or being turned into koftas. Raita made from it is also a popular local dish. The minimal cooking required for turning it into raita retains many of the nutrients, as also the flavour. It is very simple to prepare. Though somewhat similar to the cucumber raita, this one entails a little cooking of the vegetable and, thus, is less crunchy than the cucumber raita, in which the cucumber is used in its raw form.

❀ Coarsely grate the bottle gourd (*lauki*), after scraping the skin.

❀ Cook the grated gourd with the least amount of water to just allow it to become tender. As it has a lot of its own liquid, the water needed is minimal.

❀ Allow to cool.

❀ Take

Cooked, grated bottle gourd (lauki) **1 cup, 120 gm**

❀ Add it to

Yoghurt **1 cup/ 200 gm/ 200 ml**

❀ Then add

Roasted ground cumin **1 tsp/ 2 gm**
Red chilli powder **¼ tsp/ 1 gm**
Black salt (kala namak) **1tsp/ 4 gm**
Organic brown sugar (bhoori shakkar) or jaggery **a touch** (as liked)

❀ Stir well. The addition of mint leaves gives added freshness and flavour to the raita.

❀ It is a very cooling dish in the summer months.

# SPICY CARROT YOGHURT
## Gajar ka raita

PREPARATION TIME: 15 MINUTES | 2–4 SERVINGS

Yellow carrots are available here throughout the year. They are less sweet than the red ones and their colour is indicative of certain qualities they have that are different to their red sisters. While the red carrots contain a substance called lycopene, the orange and yellow ones have good amounts of xanthophyll, a naturally occurring pigment, and lutein which are linked to eye health and may help reduce the development of macular degeneration. Here, they are used in a way that would retain much of their nutrients and make them palatable. Making raita from them is a good, fresh way to serve them.

❋ Prepare

Grated carrots (grate through a medium grater)
  **1 cup/ 100 gm**

❋ It is good to grate them lengthwise to get as long strands as possible.

❋ Put 1-2 tbsp of water in a pan, add the carrots and cook on medium heat. Add a little more water, if needed, to cook the carrots till almost done but still a little crunchy. They will retain their beautiful colour. Put in a bowl and let cool. Then add some thick yoghurt, finely chopped green coriander, black salt, roasted ground cumin, a touch of organic brown sugar or tagar (boora), and red chilli powder. Now the raita is ready. The salt and spices should be used according to taste.

# Soups

To keep the system well hydrated

Soups are a welcome addition to any meal, especially in winter. At times, a hearty soup may be a good substitute for a regular meal. Soups allow the goodness of vegetables and legumes to be ingested in an easy form without the need for too much mastication! They are also good when one is not feeling one's best and there is a wish to consume something light and easily digestible. The large number of leaves, legumes, and vegetable in this region provide an opportunity for a variety of soups to be prepared.

# HIMALAYAN LENTIL AND TOMATO SOUP

### Pahadi daal aur tamatar shorba

PREPARATION TIME: 20–25 MINUTES | COOKING TIME: 25–30 MINUTES | 8 SERVINGS

Inspired by the southern Indian *rasam* and suggestions from friends, this recipe uses some local lentils, tomatoes, and *gud* for a making a hearty soup. Served with a chunky piece of bread, or rice if preferred, this can make for a meal in itself. The spicy flavour works up the system in summer and the hearty ingredients nourish the body during the cold weather.

❀ Boil together (in a pressure cooker if possible) till very mushy

Red lentil (masoor) **½ cup/ 80 gm**

Split yellow lentil (arhar daal) **½ cup/ 80 gm**

Yellow moong daal **2 tbsp/25 gm**

❀ Take

Tamarind **a lemon-sized piece/ 25 gm**

Tomatoes, chopped **4/ 225 gm**

Grated jaggery (gud) **1½ tbsp/ 12 gm**

Himalayan rock salt (saindha namak) **1-1½ tsp/ 4-6 gm**

❀ Prepare tamarind puree by soaking it in hot water for 15-20 minutes and then rubbing it well through a sieve.

❀ Add these to the daal and cook till the tomatoes are done and blended in.

❀ Add

Coarsely crushed black pepper **½ tsp/ 1 gm**

Powdered fenugreek seeds **1 tbsp/ 8 gm**

Rasam powder **1½ tbsp/ 8 gm**

Chopped coriander leaves **a bunch**

Chopped amaranth (chaulai) leaves **a small bunch**

❀ Cook for a few minutes.

❀ For the garnish, in a skillet heat

Coconut oil (organic if possible) **2 tbsp/ 20 ml**

❀ Add

Dry red chillies **2**

Mustard seeds **1 tsp/ 3 gm**

Split black gram (white urad daal) **½ tsp/ 2 gm**

Curry leaves **a few**

❀ When the ingredients splutter, add them to the daal soup and serve hot.

✎ This makes a good appetizer before a meal. May be accompanied by plain bread sticks.

# ROASTED YELLOW PUMPKIN SOUP
## Sitaphal/ kaddu shorba

PREPARATION TIME: 25–30 MINUTES | COOKING TIME: 5 MINUTES | 4–6 SERVINGS

Yellow pumpkin is available all the year round, but a hearty soup made from it is particularly welcome in the winter season. While it serves as a decorative and festive vegetable for many (as at the time of Halloween), it is actually a nutrient-dense food.

All parts of the plant - leaves, seeds, and flesh - are used in a variety of ways to gain from their nutritional value. Besides, uncut pumpkin stays fresh for a long time, so can be stored for use when not much else is available. The vegetable blends well with ginger and sweet potato. It can form a light evening meal when served with some form of bread.

Cut yellow pumpkin into large slices with skin that is well-scraped to remove the hard part and any grit that may be embedded in it. Cook on both sides in a large skillet. They will take on a mildly brownish colour from the caramellization of the sugar in it.

Yellow pumpkin **300 gm**
- In a skillet, pour 1 tbsp (5ml) olive oil and roast the pumpkin slices.

Sweet potato **100 gm**
- Wash them well, scrape, and lightly steam them. Cut these into round slices and roast lightly in a little oil.
- The same pan in which the pumpkin has been roasted can be used.

- Dry roast
Desiccated coconut **20 gm/ 5 tbsp**

- Add
Fresh ginger, grated **1 tbsp/ 10 gm**
Pink Himalayan salt **¼ tsp/ 1 gm**

- Place all three roasted ingredients in a blender and blend along with the roasted pumpkin and sweet potato. Some water may be added if too thick. Pour into a pan and bring to boil.
- Serve with a green garnish, maybe a sprig of marjoram.

Some light crackers or mathri (p. 74) would make a good accompaniment to this soup.

# HIMALAYAN SPINACH SOUP
## Pahadi palak ka shorba

PREPARATION TIME: 15 MINUTES | COOKING TIME: 10 MINUTES | 2 SERVINGS

Other than being used to prepare a variety of main dishes, *pahadi palak* is well-suited for a delectable soup. (If *pahadi palak* is not available, then other forms of spinach may be substituted.)

I took a bunch of the palak and, after washing it well and allowing the water to drain, placed the roughly broken leaves into a thick bottomed pan (a pressure cooker serves well). The cooker is covered lightly but not closed, as that would deplete the leaves of their rich colour. The leaves should be turned over after a couple of minutes of cooking to allow all of them to be lightly cooked. Soon, they will wilt and become mushy. Take off the fire and when lightly cooled, puree them in a blender. The puree can be kept in the fridge and used for varied uses.

❀ Let it brown well. Then add
Spinach puree **1 cup/ 250 gm**
Milk **½ cup/ 100 ml, or more**
Himalayan rock salt **to taste**
Black pepper **a pinch**

❀ A few sprigs of spring garlic may be added if and when available. Or some finely chopped garlic may be added when the onions turn translucent.

❀ Bring to boil and serve with a dollop of whipped cream on each cup.

🌿 Can be paired with a lavash cracker or mathri (p. 74).

❀ For the soup, place in a skillet
Olive oil **1 tsp/ 5 ml**
Butter **1 tsp/ 5 ml**

❀ Add
Finely chopped onion **1 tbsp/ 8 gm**

❀ When translucent, add
Wheat flour (atta) **1 tbsp/ 5 gm, or more**

# *Home Remedies*

## Turmeric (Haldi), Ginger (Adrak), and Basil (Tulsi)

Starting from the month of October, the makeshift roadside pop-up shops can be seen loaded with piles of fresh ginger and raw turmeric. Both grow abundantly in these environs. Other than being used extensively in many daals and vegetables, *ginger* is a popular remedy for coughs and colds, and for relieving congestion in the chest. It is used as an aid to digestion and helps relieve bloating. It is also good for relieving symptoms of nausea, especially during cancer treatment, or even motion sickness. Ginger in candied form is commonly available in many outlets. The sucking of it is a good pick-me-up. Powder made from dried ginger is used in many beverages and cool drinks to add flavour and taste and help settle the stomach, as also aid the digestive processes. It contains several anti-inflammatory and antioxidant compounds such as gingerols, beta-carotene, capsaicin, and curcumin. Good quantities of vitamin B6, magnesium, phosphorus, zinc, folate, riboflavin, and niacin contained in it make it a superfood that helps prevent many chronic disorders.

Raw *turmeric*, even though it looks like ginger, carries different qualities. The firm golden flesh encased in brownish covering, like ginger, boosts digestion, and helps relieve a bloated stomach and heartburn. It has anti-inflammatory properties that help relieve joint pains and swellings. Dry, powdered turmeric is a common ingredient in Indian food. It is also applied to injuries and wounds to help healing and stop bleeding, as it acts as an antiseptic too. For millennia, it has been a part of beauty products to bring a glow to the skin. Its blood-purifying and anti-carcinogenic abilities make it a popular daily-consumption preventive. Many people regularly drink a hot golden milk prepared by boiling it with a little turmeric powder and a pinch of black pepper. The powerful antioxidant and anti-inflammatory curcumin, an active ingredient in turmeric, is better released and absorbed when combined with black pepper.

L to R: Tulsi, ginger and raw turmeric

**As a relish:** In its raw form, turmeric can be cut into fine juliennes, together with fresh ginger, and preserved in a glass jar with some lemon juice, a little vinegar, pink Himalayan salt, and some red or green chillies thrown in. It stays for long in the refrigerator and makes for a good zesty addition to any meal. Both ingredients help the digestive processes, even as they provide antiseptic and anti-inflammatory substances to the body.

*Basil* or tulsi, known to be a royal herb, is looked upon as a powerful plant in most cultures. In India, recognizing its many qualities, it is worshipped as a holy plant. It is seen to be an incarnation of Goddess Lakshmi, hence very dear to Lord Vishnu. It is also said to represent Radha, a symbol of unconditional love. It is often grown in a particular part of the courtyard and watered every day, as a form of oblation to the Divine. Other cultures have other beliefs with regard to this fragrant plant. An African legend claims that basil protects one against scorpions, while a French myth proclaims that smelling basil too much would breed scorpions in the brain! Either way, it is not a herb that can be ignored.

All parts of the minty, pungent plant are good for different parts of the body and have high therapeutic value. It is said to contain high quantities of vitamin A and C, calcium, zinc, iron, and chlorophyll. It is also seen to be a disinfectant, a panacea for respiratory disorders, and has a calming effect on the nerves. I remember, once when, as a child, I developed fever, my grandmother gave me tulsi tea, which rid me of the malady in a day or two. A good mood booster, it is also a skin cleanser.

I have five varieties of the herb in my little garden, and each one carries a different pungency and aroma. I have the usual *rama* and *shyama* tulsis, and I have lemon tulsi and *murua* tulsi, also called sweet basil. It makes the whole area fragrant with its sweet smell. One other variety was brought by my music teacher. It has bigger leaves and a much milder flavour than the others. Many a time, I use a blend of all of them to prepare a sauce to enhance the flavours of certain vegetables and, of course, pasta.

# Chutneys
To add zest to the meal

The hills abound in ingredients that can be used directly, in their raw form, and sometimes even cooked lightly to act as appetizers and digestive food. These ingredients may carry nutrients not found in other foods, thus adding to the resources of the body. The chutneys, made from such ingredients, not only enhance taste and zest, but help the absorption of other foods that are ingested in the main meal. Chutneys can be had on their own with rice or rotis, even as a substitute for vegetables or daal, in case there is not enough time to cook those. Most chutneys stay fresh for a few days, especially when kept in the fridge. Some particular chutneys are very popular in this region and are prepared extensively. Various seeds, herbs, and even legumes can make interesting additions to the food.

# CREAMY COCONUT CHUTNEY
## Nariyal ki mazedaar chutney

PREPARATION TIME: 15–20 MINUTES

Coconut allows for many kinds of experimentation, even as it adds flavour and nutrients to various food. Interestingly, other than the sweet flavour, a 2 X 2 piece of fresh coconut meat contains only about 7 grams of carbohydrate (much less than what we may get from a medium-sized apple) and provides us with 4 grams of fibre (a large percentage of our daily requirement). Even though it contains a good amount of saturated fat, much of this fat is seen to contain an element called 'lauric' acid, which can actually boost the 'good' cholesterol levels and help reduce the risk of heart disease. But one need not go overboard with coconut consumption, even though it provides a number of trace elements such as copper, calcium, iron, manganese, magnesium, and zinc.

❀ **Grind together**

Fresh grated coconut **10 tbsp/ 75 gm**

Green chilli **1**

Roasted peanuts **3 tbsp/ 30 gm**

Fresh ginger **2 tbsp/ 20 gm**

Water **1 tbsp/ 10 ml**

Yoghurt **2 tbsp/ 25 gm**

Pink Himalayan salt **1 tsp/ 4 gm**

Ground roasted cumin (jeera)
   **1 tsp/ 2 gm**

Peanut oil **1 tbsp/ 10 ml**

Mustard seeds, lightly roasted
   **1 tsp/ 3 gm**

Grated jaggery (gud) **1 tsp/ 4 gm**

❀ The chutney will stay well for 3-4 days
   in the fridge.

Coconut chutney (this goes well with idli, dosa or chilla).

# BEEFSTEAK PLANT AND BLACK SOYABEANS CHUTNEY
## Bhangjeera aur kaale bhatt ki chutney

PREPARATION TIME: 15 MINUTES

The aromatic seeds of *bhangjeera (Perilla frutescens)* are used as a spice for flavouring food as also for making nutritious chutneys. Though bearing the word 'bhang' in its name, it has nothing to do with bhang drawn from the cannabis plant. It does not have any hallucinatory qualities. In English, for some reason it is called 'beefsteak plant'! Found in the upper Himalayan regions, *bhangjeera* seeds are rich in Omega 3 and Omega 6 fatty acids. They are known to be a better source of these fatty acids than cod liver oil, and are said to help reduce inflammations and also prevent heart ailments. The seeds are often used as a spice when cooking certain vegetables or daals. The leaves of the *bhangjeera* shrubs are known to treat cough, cold, asthma, and certain food allergies.

*Kaale bhatt*, or black soyabeans, are also sourced from the upper regions of Uttarakhand. Extremely rich in proteins and iron, they provide a number of essential amino acids. Soya protein is known to lower cholesterol levels considerably. The locals prepare a soupy daal from it by boiling it together with some other legumes like *gehat (kulath)* and chickpea. In some parts of Uttarakhand, they make a dish called *churdakni* by cooking it together with atta (wheat) flour or rice flour. The most popular is the delectable chutney made from lightly roasted seeds. Taking a cue from the locals, I devised my own.

❀ Grind together in a blender
Lightly roasted Himalayan
    black soyabeans (kaale bhatt) **4 tbsp/ 50 gm**
Bhangjeera, lightly warmed on a hot tawa
    **3 tbsp/ 20 gm**
Dried red chilli **1**

❀ Add to this
Himalayan pink salt **½ tsp/ 2 gm**
Black salt **½ tsp/ 2 gm**
Fresh curry leaves (kadi patta) **6-8**
Green chilli **1**

❀ Add to this a handful of assorted fresh basil
    leaves (can be a combination of sweet basil,
    lemon basil, and the usual *rama* and *shyama*
    tulsis).
Fresh oregano (ajwain) leaves **5**

❀ If available, some mint or arugula leaves
    may be added.
Fresh marjoram **1 sprig**

❀ If not available, commercially available
    dried marjoram may be added, or even
    omitted altogether.
Peanut oil (or any other oil of choice)
    **1 tbsp/ 10ml**
Water **5 tbsp/ 50 ml**
    (or more if you prefer a thinner, liquid
    consistency)

❀ The chutney pairs well with steamed or
    roasted vegetables. It can, of course, be had
    with rotis or rice.

🌿 Can be paired with your favourite stuffed
    paratha.

Black soybeans (*kale bhatt*)
Image Source: Veganbaking.net/ Wikimedia Commons / CC BY-SA 2.0

# INDIAN GOOSEBERRY AND APPLE CHUTNEY
## Amla aur sev ki chutney

### PREPARATION TIME: 15–20 MINUTES

There are a number of *amla* (Indian gooseberry or myrobalan) trees near our residential complex. In the months of October–November, the trees provide bountiful harvests of the green, juicy, astringent berries containing a hard seed inside. Known to be a wonder fruit, *amla* carries very high quantities of vitamin C, potassium, calcium, magnesium, iron, fibre, and other ingredients that are known to uproot a number of diseases. In the science of Ayurveda, *amla* is looked upon as a life-giving elixir. Some ingredients in it help strengthen the heart, lower cholesterol, maintain strong bones, and sharpen the capacity of the eyes. The fruit is used in a number of Ayurvedic remedies, the most famous preparation being *chyavan praash*. The fresh berries can be used for zesty digestive chutneys. Some people also cook it as a vegetable.

The apple I used came from Harsil, in the upper regions of Uttarakhand. The disease-fighting phytonutrients in apples help maintain bodily health. Their anti-oxidative, anti-inflammatory properties are said to help reduce the risk of cancer.

❀ **Grind well together**

Indian gooseberry (amla) **4**
  (Cut the flesh off the seed into small pieces)
Apple, chopped and seeds removed **1**
Green chilli **1**
Fresh lemon juice **1 tbsp/ 5 gm**
Organic brown sugar (bhoori shakkar)
  **2 tsp/ 8 gm**
Pink Himalayan salt **2 tsp/ 8 gm**
Roasted cumin powder **2 tsp/ 4 gm**

❀ The chutney stays fresh for a couple of weeks in the fridge.

  May be paired with some dry vegetable and paratha.

# HEMP SEED CHUTNEY
## Bhang chutney

PREPARATION TIME: 15 MINUTES

Bhang chutney is a very popular add-on in the Garhwal region. The seeds have a nutty, crispy taste and many locals add them to their pakoras or crisps. We combined it with some pungent and peppery arugula (rocket) leaves. Other than boosting the immune system and helping absorption of minerals in the body, it is supposed to strengthen the brain.

Hemp seeds (bhang) lightly roasted **¼ cup/ 30 gm**

Arugula, if available, or use any other leaves like coriander, mint, or cilantro **10-12 leaves**

Some other leaves like basil, marjoram sprigs, etc. may be added **a few of each**

Fresh ginger **1" cube/ 20 gm**

Green chillies **2**

Himalayan pink salt **½ tsp/ 2 gm**

Black salt **½ tsp/ 2 gm**

Dried pomegranate seed (anardana) powdered **1 tsp/ 2 gm**

Organic brown sugar (bhoori shakkar) **1 tsp/ 4 gm**

Lemon juice **1 tbsp/ 10 gm**

❀ Grind all together to a nice paste. Add water to gain the desired consistency.

⟶ Spread on thinly sliced toasted flavoured bread.

# DRIED DATE AND FENUGREEK CHUTNEY
## Chhuare aur methi ki chutney

PREPARATION TIME: 15 MINUTES + SOAKING TIME | COOKING TIME: 15 MINUTES

Methi (fenugreek) seeds are an important Ayurvedic remedy for several ailments. Packed with health-giving nutrients, the bitter, pungent fenugreek has been used since millennia for various skin-improving potions. They are also known to promote hair growth. The flavour-enhancing seeds are beneficial for disorders such as indigestion or constipation. They are also used for regulating blood sugar levels. They help the absorption of some foods that otherwise maybe a little hard to digest. Methi seeds sprout well and can be added to salads and sprouted beans, etc.

In this chutney, the bitter and pungent flavours of the methi and ginger blend well with the sweetness of dried dates, *chhuara*, which are a storehouse of

energy-giving elements. The vitamins they are known to contain range from A, C, E, K, B2, B6, including niacin and thiamin. They carry essential minerals like iron, potassium, selenium, magnesium, phosphorous, and copper to help our body cells perform their work. Consumption of dates in one form or another goes a long way in maintaining overall energy levels. They are also known to be a good remedy for dry eye and dry mouth syndromes.

The benefits of methi and *chhuara*, combined with the anti-inflammatory and antioxidant compounds, such as gingerols, beta-carotene, capsaicin, and curcumin among others, found in ginger, make this chutney a superfood that should be kept in one's fridge at all times, as it goes well with everything and stays for long.

※ Soak dates (chhuara) in a little water for 5-6 hours (or more if too dry) and then cut into thin slices discarding the pits. Retain the water
Dried dates (chhuara) **12**

※ Also soak in water for 5-6 hours (do not throw away the water)
Fenugreek (methi) seeds **5 tbsp/ 20 gm**

※ Heat in a skillet
Mustard oil **2 tbsp/ 20 ml**

※ Add
Wild mustard (jakhiya) **1 tsp/ 2 gm**

※ Let splutter, then add
Coarsely grated ginger **about 7 tbsp/ 70 gm**

※ Cook for a few minutes and add the soaked methi seeds. Add the dates (chhuara). Cook for 2-3 minutes. Then add

Grated jaggery (gud) **6 tbsp / 50 gm**
Vinegar **1½ tbsp/ 15-20ml**
Water **½ cup/ 100 ml, or more**

※ The water in which the chhuaras and the methi seeds were soaked can also be added.
※ The chutney will be moist but not watery.

🌾 May be tried with kababs, fritters or chillas.

## SEMI-DRY CRUNCHY LENTILS CHUTNEY

Daal aur sarsondana ki sookhi chutney

PREPARATION TIME: 20–25 MINUTES

This chutney gives a nice crunchy flavour to roasted (or steamed) vegetables, like zucchini and sweet potato, even as it provides all the goodness of the legumes that go into it. Other than flavour, this chutney adds valuable proteins and micronutrients, that help the system improve its bowel function. The fibre in these lentils helps to maintain a healthy gut, thus enabling better absorption of glucose, which helps better brain function.

- ❀ On a dry tawa, roast each one separately till lightly browned

Red, yellow lentils, and Bengal gram (moong, masoor or malka, arhar, and chana daals) **1 tbsp/1-½ gms each**

- ❀ Roast together

Dry red chilli **1**

Black mustard seeds **¼ tsp/1 gm**

Yellow mustard seeds **¼ tsp/1 gm**

- ❀ Powder all in a spice or coffee grinder.
- ❀ Add Himalayan pink salt (to taste) while grinding.
- ❀ Then add a few finely chopped sprigs of spring garlic (optional).
- ❀ Add enough mustard oil to make the mixture reach a gooey consistency.

## PESTO'ISH

PREPARATION TIME: 15–20 MINUTES

This is a pesto-type sauce made from fresh leaves and seeds abundantly available here. Instead of the pine nuts used in regular pesto, *chironji* (cuddapah almond) has been used, which is easier to find and has a nutty flavour like a mix of almonds and walnuts, while being soft like pine nuts. Ground together with rose water, the seeds make for a highly beneficial face pack. Other than this, *chironji* is helpful in preventing bloating of the abdomen due to gaseous formations. It also helps regulate diarrhoea and is rich in Vitamin B.

- ❀ Lightly roast (just enough to release their flavours)

Beefsteak plant seeds (bhangjeera) **4 tbsp/20 gm**

Cuddapah almond (chironji) **4 tbsp/40 gm**

- ❀ Grind the two in a coffee grinder. Add small handfuls/ bunches of arugula (fresh green leaves like rocket leaves used for salads), mint, sweet basil, lemon basil, 2 green chillies, and pink Himalayan salt and grind further. Make sure that all the greens are well-washed and cleaned. Add a little lemon juice.
- ❀ Add olive oil, little by little, and blend. Add as much of the oil as would give the desired consistency. A touch of organic brown sugar (bhoori shakkar) may be added if liked.

⤛ The sauce is great with pasta, vegetables, bread, or parathas.

Pesto'ish

L to R: Poppy seeds, hemp and amaranth

**K**hus khus is a popular ingredient in Indian cooking. Other than adding an amazing flavour to certain dishes, *khus khus* is rich in proteins and Omega-6 fatty acids and so is beneficial for the immune system. It also has properties that prevent crystallization of excess calcium in the body, thus helping to prevent kidney stones. Since it contains very small amounts of opium alkaloids, it is helpful in inducing a good sleep. It can also help reduce irritability, as it soothes tensed nerves and acts as pain reliever. *Khus khus* also has a role in beauty culture. It acts as cosmetic corrective by helping to maintain a healthy skin.

*Bhang*, a variety of the cannabis plant, grows all over on the hills around. It carries negligible amounts of the intoxicating THC found in marijuana. It is believed to contain healthy fats, proteins, and several minerals such as phosphorus, potassium, sodium, magnesium, sulphur, calcium, iron, and zinc. Bhang seeds also help in relieving joint and arthritic pains.

The gamma-linolenic acid in it is supposed to be helpful for people suffering from diabetes or heart disease. It is effective in preventing some skin allergies too.

*Chaulai*, or amaranth, is a high-protein grain. It is also called *rajgira*, royal grain, or superfood due to the high concentration of essential vitamins and minerals it has. Its high dietary fibre content improves the digestive system and reduces cholesterol, thus helping to improve cardiovascular health. It is known to have a higher calcium content than milk. Vitamins A and C in it help boost immune system and improve the health of eyes. It is good for weight loss diets. This also works as a beauty product, as it strengthens the hair and makes them more lustrous.

# Foods that Soothe

## For a deeper satisfaction

**W**hile all foods provide satisfaction, there are some that one tends to sit down and relax with, or they may have a quality that imbues one with a sense of contentment and unexplainable joy. These foods often tend to be high in fat, dense energy, and sugar. They may be foods that immediately connect one with the bounty and sweetness of nature, which otherwise may go somewhat unnoticed. They may even evoke some deep-seated memories or cause one to savour the love of the one who prepared it - that may be the reason why our mothers' cooking is special. At different times, different foods serve these different functions. However, comforting, soothing foods can also be healthy and nourishing.

# BARNYARD MILLET PUDDING
## Himalayan jhangore ki kheer

PREPARATION TIME: 5 MINUTES  |  COOKING TIME: 20–25 MINUTES  |  4 SERVINGS

*Jhangora* or 'barnyard millet', is a light-textured seed used in many ways in the hills of Uttarkhand. Its versatility lends itself to being used for non-semolina *upama* preparation, or even for light pulaos. It can be dry-roasted and then plunged into boiling water to make a tabbouleh for a wholesome salad. Here, we suggest a light kheer – an indigenous local pudding easier to digest than the usual rice kheer and taking less time to cook – that would appeal to the gastronome's palate.

For the kheer, I used full-cream milk without prior boiling and without removing the creamy layer. The sweetening was done with *gud*, which provides its own aroma to the dish. It is better to add the *gud* at the end, as it may curdle the milk if added too early. Even then, if it gives it a mildly curdled look, it is quite okay as it provides a nice texture.

❀ To prepare, put aside
Himalayan barnyard millet (jhangora),
   well washed **½ cup/ 100 gm**

❀ Bring to a boil
Full-cream milk **2½ cups/ 500 ml, or more**

❀ Add jhangora to the milk. Stir from time to time and let cook till thick and the jhangora looks translucent. It will take on a thick creamy look. Add
Raisins **1 tbsp/ 10 gm**
Cuddapah almonds (chironji) **1 tbsp/ 10 gm**
Crushed cardamoms **3 whole**
Few strands saffron, soaked in **½ tsp water**

❀ Mix well. Then add
Grated jaggery (gud) **½ cup/ 90 gm**

❀ Let it melt into the mixture for a couple of minutes. The kheer has a light and delicate texture and may be served hot or cold with a sprinkling of flaked pistachios or roasted sunflower or pumpkin seeds or any other garnish of choice.

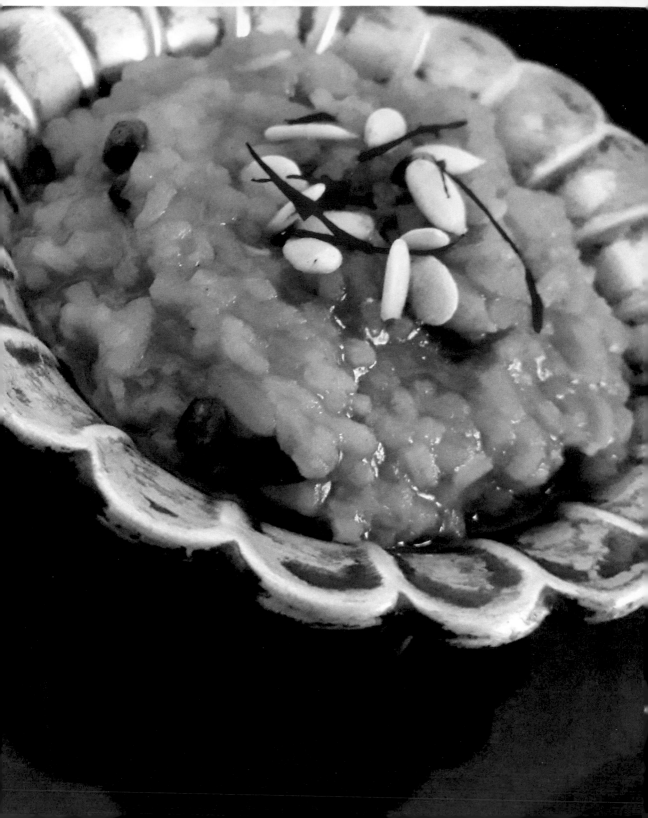

# RICE PUDDING IN SUGARCANE JUICE
## Ganne ki kheer

**PREPARATION TIME: 5 MINUTES | COOKING TIME: 20–25 MINUTES | 2 SERVINGS**

The streets of Rishikesh can be seen studded with carts selling sugarcane juice almost all year round. But from about October, one sees a greater abundance of these. Each cart carries large bundles of the reed along with a hand-operated crushing wheel that works almost continuously to cater to eager consumers. The addition of fresh ginger, lemon juice, and some mild spices makes the juice even more delectable. Other than being tasty and refreshing, the alkaline super fluid is rich in electrolytes such as calcium, magnesium, potassium, iron, and manganese and is also known to be a liver cleanser. It helps to quickly replenish the nutrients lost by the body while coping with various antigens that are ingested into it in the process of living. It is supposed to help fight certain types of cancer, as the disease cannot survive in an alkaline environment. Its slow release of sugar into the blood helps keep the sugar levels regulated.

Other than being served as a refreshing drink, the juice is used for making *gud* and *khand* and the chemically refined sugar we use on our tables. The residual fibre is used as fuel or even for making paper. It also goes into the making of certain types of alcohol.

❀ For the kheer, we need
Broken rice ¼ cup/ 50 gm

❀ Put it on to simmer with
Water 1 cup/ 220 ml
❀ Soon, it will soften while still being slightly uncooked. Then pour in
Sugarcane juice 1 cup/ 220 ml

❀ Let it cook till the rice is completely soft and blended with the sugarcane juice to a thick viscous and pudding-like texture. A little taste gave me the idea of how much more juice to add for sweetness and also how much more to cook so that the rice may be creamy soft and the kheer viscous enough to be pleasing when tasted.
❀ Even without adding any other ingredient like nuts or cardamom, the kheer was delectable as it carried a full-bodied flavour of the sugarcane.

# CARROT AND MILK PUDDING
## Gajar ka halwa

PREPARATION TIME: 10–15 MINUTES | COOKING TIME: 30-35 MINUTES | 4–6 SERVINGS

In Rishikesh, we mostly get yellowy-orange-coloured carrots as against the beautiful red ones in the plains. It is in winter that we get the deep red ones that go into the making of halwa.

Carrots gain their orange or red colour from the beta-carotene, which gets converted into vitamin A in the body. They are a good source of fibre. The soluble fibre in them helps lower blood sugar levels by slowing down digestion of sugars and starches. The insoluble fibre promotes healthy bowels. Carrots lend themselves to varied preparations. They are a good addition to the diet in any form.

❀ For the halwa, take a saucepan or kadai and heat milk in it till it reaches near boiling point.
Full-cream milk **500 gm/½ litre**

❀ Grate carrots with a medium grater. Add the grated carrots to the milk after it starts bubbling softly.
Grated carrots **5 cups/ 500 gm**

❀ Let cook on low heat. Stir from time to time to prevent sticking as also boiling over.

Continue cooking till the water evaporates and the mixture attains a semi-dry consistency. Add the following ingredients to the milk and the carrots
Washed raisins **3 tbsp/ 30 gm**
Fresh cream (malai) **3 tbsp/ 30 gm**
Grated jaggery (boora may be used if preferred over gud) **6 tbsp/ 50 gm**
Slivered almonds **6**
Crushed cardamoms with skin **3**

❀ Cook for 5-10 minutes. Add 5-10 saffron strands that may have been soaked in a tsp of milk for 10-15 minutes. Garnish with desired nuts.

# MANGO FOOL
## Aam ras

PREPARATION TIME: 10 MINUTES | 2 SERVINGS

The summer season brings on the king of fruits in all its variety. Many memories of varied kinds are connected with mangoes in most minds. A juicy sweet variety with a slight tang was used – this time a *chausa* variety of mango (other preferred varieties can be tried) – for recreating a semblance of what I had in my childhood (a dessert often made by my mother). This is simple, quick, and delicious version even as it retains the freshness and the flavour of the fruit. It stays well for a couple of days in the fridge.

❀ Blend together
Fresh mango puree  **1 cup/ 250 gm**
Fresh malai  **2 tbsp/ 20 gm**
Lemon juice  **1 tsp/ 5 gm**
Lemon zest  **¼ tsp/ ½ gm**
Organic brown sugar (boora)  **1 tsp/ 5 gm**

❀ Pour into small glass bowls for serving and garnish with sprigs of fresh peppermint leaves.

✺ May be served with some light wafers.

# ALMOST MALPUA
## Daal-chawal ka malpua

8–10 SERVINGS

Christmas time always made my Jharkhandi house help, Sarita, very busy. Much to my discomfiture and chagrin, she would always take off for more days than she committed herself to. On one of her returns, she came back with a stack of dosa-like goodies, different to similar-looking savoury preparation that I had had before. The sweet dish she brought was delicious and turned me into a participant in her celebrations. I could not but laugh with her for her usual delay.

Dosa, to me, had been a salty, spicy fermented flat bread that makes a nice snack or a meal. But this one was sweet and soft. It could be eaten without any accompaniment, as a satisfying snack. She taught me two versions of it. Both quite different in the quality of satiation they provided.

One was a blend of rice and *urad* daal. Uttarakhandis use *urad* daal to prepare crunchy vadas, a favoured delicacy during the monsoon season. Actually, vadas, in some form or another, are a common preparation all across India. This preparation allowed me to use the daal in a different way – as a sweet preparation.

## The first version

PREPARATION TIME: 15–20 MINUTES + FERMENTATION FOR 4-5 HOURS + SOAKTIME | COOKING TIME: 15-20 MINUTES

Rice, soaked in a little water overnight **1 cup/ 200 gm**

Urad daal, soaked overnight **¼ cup/ 40 gm** (They can also be soaked in the morning and ground in the evening.)

❀ Grind the two separately the next morning, then mix together to form a smooth batter.

❀ Into that, add

Jaggery (gud) **1½ tbsp/ 12 gm** (more gud may be added if desired after tasting one prepared dosa)

137

- ❀ This needs to be left for 4-5 hours till well fermented (if the ambient temperature is cool, the fermenting process may take longer. Some bubbles will be visible on the fermented batter).
- ❀ Add water to make the blend into a nice pourable consistency.
- ❀ Then spread out the batter thinly with a ladle, pancake-like, on a non-stick skillet and cook with a little oil (preferably peanut or coconut oil) till golden brown on one side. Then flip and let the other side cook. And voila, it is ready!

## The second version

PREPARATION TIME: 15–20 MINUTES |
COOKING TIME: 20-25 MINUTES

- ❀ It calls for equal quantities of white flour (maida) and sooji (semolina). The two are made into a pourable batter with milk and some sugar (gud can be used too).
- ❀ I made a still different, more localized, version and used

Semolina **½ cup/ 75 gm**

Himalayan finger millet (mandua) flour
**¼ cup/ 25 gm**

Wheat flour (atta) **¼ cup/ 30 gm**

(these last two were substitutes for the maida)

- ❀ To this mixture, I added

Salt **a pinch**

Red chilli powder **a pinch**

Milk **¾ cup/ 170 ml**

Grated jaggery (gud) **¼ cup/ 45 gm**

- ❀ The consistency should be like that of pancake mixture. Let the mixture stand for at least ½ hour. It then gains a sort of creamy texture. Spread it on a lightly oiled non-stick skillet in the shape of small malpuas, or pancakes. Cook on both sides till lightly browned. The gud gives it a mildly crispy texture.
- ❀ The batter can also be ladled into thick dumpling-like blobs, in a quarter-inch layer of oil in the pan, and allowed to cook till done right through. Some anise seeds may be added to the dumplings if liked. The malpua version and the dumpling versions carry different tastes.
- ❀ If placed in the fridge, they will keep well for 5-6 days. They can be re-heated in a skillet as and when needed.

Jaggery cubes

Image Source: Mangosapiens/
Wikimedia Commons / CC BY-SA 4.0

# PHONY/SHAM GULAB JAMUN
## Banawati gulab jamun

PREPARATION TIME: 15 MINUTES | COOKING TIME: 20 MINUTES | 8 SERVINGS

The Jharkhandi kitchen help also taught me how to quickly make gulab jamuns, which do not require great expertise, are lighter, and provide a nice sense of satiation.

Regular gulab jamuns are made from white flour (maida) and *khoya* (milk cooked till it forms a dry consistency) and soaked in heavy syrup. They tend to be heavy and call for more work by the digestive system. In these gulab jamuns, one may use a healthy bread, one that does not have a grainy texture so that it may bind well. The addition of flaxseeds for binding adds to the nutritional quality of the dish. It is best to keep the sugar syrup somewhat light.

❀ You will need

Bread **8 slices**

❀ These can be from some old bread that may have been stored away and forgotten in the freezer. Crumble the slices into soft crumbs along with their crust.

❀ Add to this

Rice flour **2 tbsp/ 20 gm**

Semolina (sooji) **1 tbsp/ 10 gm**

Tagar (boora) **2 tbsp/ 15 gm**

Flaxseeds (alsi), coarsely ground **1 tbsp/ 10 gm**, soaked in water **3 tbsp**

Fresh cream (malai) **2 tbsp/ 20 gm**

❀ Mix well and add

Milk **1-2 tbsp/ 10-20 gm**, depending on how moist the bread is, to knead the bread into a firm but soft dough.

❀ Make small balls (the size of large marbles) and fry in peanut or other oil of choice. These jamuns do not soak much oil. A small quantity of dough suffices for a whole lot.

❀ Prepare a syrup by boiling coarse sugar in water.

Tagar, coarse sugar (boora) or sugar **1 cup/ 140 gm**

Water **2 cups/ 220 ml**

❀ Bring the mixture to boil and let simmer for about five minutes. Add some green cardamoms to the sugar syrup for flavour. Let the syrup cool lightly before putting the jamuns into it. They are lighter, and even tastier than the traditional gulab jamuns.

❀ Though boora is made from sugar, it is tastier and healthier. The process of preparation makes boora more porous and absorbent as compared to just powdered sugar. It is absorbed into the blood more slowly than sugar, hence is healthier. Boora mixed with ghee is a delectable addition to plain boiled rice. It can also be had with roti or paratha.

# As They Walk Along

Rishikesh is one of the most, if not the most, visited places of pilgrimage in India. Devotees from all parts of India and the world come for a darshan of the sacred river Ganga or to visit and learn at the various ashramas, some of the oldest in India. The area from Haridwar to Rishikesh, and further up, is particularly sacred. As the name suggests, Hari or Hardwar is the gateway to Vishnu or Shiva - the most favoured gods of the Hindu pantheon. It is here that the river Ganga spreads out to allow the faithful to take an auspicious dip and pray to the holiest of the holy.

Rishikesh, meaning the lord or the conqueror of the sense organs, has been a place sanctified by sages who meditated here. Their energy, still felt in the humdrum of day-to-day life here, is what draws people to this place now named the 'Yoga Capital of the World'. Once visited, most people come back attracted by the magnetic energy of the place.

Pilgrims for a ritual darshan

Rishikesh is also the gateway to the sacred Chardham - Gangotri, Yamunotri, Kedar, and Badri. Anyone wishing to visit those must pass through this hallowed town, savour its sanctity, and proceed. As such, it attracts pilgrims of all hues and colours. There are the orthodox devout who come this way as part of completing some valued religious rituals, there are the faithful who do not wish to miss out on a darshan of the sacred shrines while still in this life form, and there are the eager aspirants who wish to learn at the feet of some enlightened ones. A great majority are the non-intellectually inclined religious people who come with the deepest of faith, walking great distances just to carry some Ganga water or prasad from a shrine they revere and take it back to their place of origin. Certain times of the year are seen to be especially auspicious for performing such yatras. The month of Shravana, which falls during the rainy season, is more auspicious than others for such an undertaking. Arriving sometime in July and August, this month is witness to millions of *yatris*, many walking all the way on foot, others using whatever form of transport they can find. The authorities have to make special arrangements to facilitate the walkers and other pilgrims, so that they are not hindered by the regular heavy traffic. The enormous crowds, sporting the various colours and attires of their states, towns, and villages, represent a mini India as they mingle, drawn by their beliefs. Devotion and faith become levelers of all differences as all resolve into one sentient mass seeking to make a connection with the Divine.

Many of the walkers carry, or pick up along the way, some easy-to-eat foods that can be consumed as they walk along tirelessly. The following recipes have been presented with some variations, taking cues from that which is seen along the roads.

*Moongphalis* for sale

# PUFFED RICE
## Murmura

PREPARATION TIME: 5 MINUTES | COOKING TIME: 5–10 MINUTES | 6 SERVINGS

*Murmura*, or puffed rice, is a popular street food in India. It is prepared in a special way by heating white rice on high temperature till it puffs and becomes somewhat crunchy. Actually, on its own, *murmura* has little nutritional value. It has some trace minerals and negligible amounts of carbohydrates and protein. Its high glycemic index also does not render it a very sustaining food. It is the addition of other ingredients, such as chickpeas, peanuts or sesame that give it nutritional strength and also make it into a food that provides satisfaction, and a sense of fullness, for a longer period of time. *Murmura* remains a tasty and desired in-between-meals snack. It is also a good carry-along food for journeys as it is light and delectable. As *murmura* absorbs moisture very quickly, it calls for being stored in air-tight packs.

In a wok like skillet, heat the following ingredients one by one, in the same order. The mustard oil should be adequately hot and smoking before the gas is turned down to medium and dry red chillies are added. Sugar should be added after the spices and seeds stop spluttering.

Mustard oil **1 tbsp / 10 ml**
Dried red chillies **2 whole**
Black mustard seeds **1 tsp / 3 gm**
Yellow mustard seeds **1 tsp / 3 gm**
Cumin (jeera), whole **1 tsp / 5 gm**
Brown sugar (bhoori shakkar) **1 tsp / 4 gm**
Salt **to taste**
Whole curry leaves (kadhi patta), fresh or dry **10-12**

Roasted chickpeas (chana) **¾ cup / 70 gm**
Roasted peanuts **¾ cup / 80 gm**
Roasted sesame (optional) **½ cup / 80 gm**

❀ Mix well, cool, and store in an airtight container.

✥ A good snack with some fresh lemon drink.

❀ The seeds will splutter, the sugar will melt, and all spices will get mixed together.
❀ Then add
Puffed rice (murmura) **3 cups / 60 gm**

❀ Stir till crispy and well mixed with the spices. Add

# AMARANTH SEED AND JAGGERY BALLS
## Rajgira aur gud ke laddoo

PREPARATION TIME: 5 MINUTES | COOKING TIME: 15–20 MINUTES | MAKES 10–12 BALLS

These nutritious laddoos are highly sustaining while being delectable. Prepared with *rajgira*, chia, sesame, and puffed rice (*murmura*), they carry the goodness of three seeds, which makes them high in calcium, fibre, and other micronutrients. Amaranth is rich in protein and fibres and carries high amounts of micronutrients like manganese, iron, phosphorus, magnesium, and also copper. It is, thus, seen to be a good brain food. The leaves make for a nutritious saag. The seeds can be ground into flour for use in various ways. Laddoos made from it act as a good and satisfying carry-along snack. This recipe can be vegan if ghee is replaced with oil.

❀ Roast on a skillet.

Amaranth seeds (rajgira) **½ cup/ 90 g**

❀ Wait till they pop and puff open like minute popcorn.

❀ The seeds should be placed little by little on an already well-heated skillet. Shake or stir them continuously. The heat may be reduced after a while to allow them to pop fully. Even so, several seeds will not pop open but will become crunchy and flavourful.

❀ Add

Puffed rice (murmura)
(lightly roasted to make it crisp) **1 cup/ 20 gm**

Sesame seeds lightly roasted to release flavour **¼ cup/ 40 gm**

Hemp (bhang) seeds (optional) **¼ cup/ 30 gm**

❀ Roast them very lightly. Place them in a coffee grinder and whirl for 5 seconds to break the seeds.

Chia **¼ cup/ 40 gm**

❀ Heat in a pan with some water

Grated jaggery (gud) **½ cup/ 90 gm**

❀ Add

Ghee **1 tsp/ 5 ml**

❀ Turn off heat. Then add the dry ingredients to the jaggery and ghee mix.

❀ Let it cool a little. Then with hands dipped in cool water, make little balls and let dry.

❀ These would stay well for a few weeks.

✿ Good with a cup of masala chai.

# WATER CHESTNUT
## Singhara

PREPARATION TIME: 10 MINUTES | COOKING TIME: 5–10 MINUTES | 4 SERVINGS

*Singharas* or water chestnuts are actually tubers that grow in swampy and marshy lands. They come into the market around the time of Navaratri – nine days dedicated to the worship of the Divine Feminine. This amazing vegetable forms an important and nutritious part of the fasting diets that many people follow during this time. This is a diet in which cereal foods are generally avoided and are replaced by seeds, vegetables, and fruits. It thus becomes a time for cleansing the system and giving it a rest from the usual heavy foods, which require some hard work from the digestive apparatus. A high-volume food, this vegetable is almost 75 per cent water. It gives a sense of fullness for long and can be a good weight-loss food. Flour made from dried *singhara* is used during this period for making sumptuous rotis, puris, or halwas. Like many such foods, this vegetable – which is actually not a nut at all – contains high amounts of fibre, potassium, manganese, and copper. It also contains good amounts of vitamin B6 and riboflavin. It contains antioxidants that protect the body.

The tuber, when peeled, reveals a heart-shaped, crisp, white fruit. Though it can be eaten raw, it is advised to not do so, as it grows in places that may be full of harmful bacteria. One can steam it whole, peel it when a little cool, and sprinkle it with some salt and pepper. Chaat masala may be used if liked. It is a good, nutritious, and easy-to-eat item to carry when walking or travelling.

- ❀ Slit water chestnuts lengthwise and scoop out the flesh with a sharp knife.

Water chestnut (singhara) **250 gms**

- ❀ Sautée them in a few drops of oil till lightly browned and sprinkle them with salt and pepper. It gives a fresh crisp taste, modifying the water chestnuts into a tasty, carry-along snack, or a side dish that can be served with soup, or even added to salads.

- ⟜ Can also be had as a hot snack with a refreshing drink

# *Air Plant or Dard Maar*
## The Miracle Leaf

Not too far into the cookbook, my aide Nandita stepped into one of the hundreds of potholes on the road and hobbled in severe pain. I helped her soak the foot in warm water and sea salt with bicarbonate of soda thrown in, then tied a crepe bandage on it after applying some pain-relieving unguent, as I could not have my 'lab assistant' out of action for too long. Just then the '*dard maar*' leaf in my balcony beckoned to me. Vidhata, my Uttarakhandi helper, had brought the plant some months ago, and its leaves had now come into full-blown form.

I decided to test its capacity. After helping with the foot-soaking, I prepared the leaf by heating half a teaspoon of mustard oil (*sarson ka tel*), with half a teaspoon of turmeric (*haldi*), on a flat griddle (*tawa*). When both were nicely hot, I turned off the heat and placed a couple of leaves on the oily mixture face-down.

Air plant or *Dard Maar*

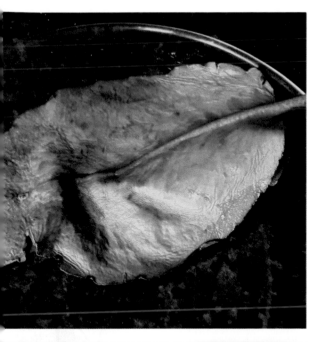

I placed the warm leaves on the swollen ankle and tied them down with the crepe bandage. After 10-12 hours, when we opened the bandage for another application, we found to our amazement that the ankle which had grown to the size of a lemon had now shrunk down to about 40 per cent of what it was. The pain was less. That which I could not touch earlier without making her wince was now amenable to touch.

Surprised, we explored, trying to find out more about the leaf. Sure enough, in popular parlance, it is given names like miracle leaf, magic leaf, air plant. I now have more respect for this plant, which, other than adding beauty to my little garden, also provides a healing touch.

# In the End

It is now evident that more than *how much* we put into our mouths, it is *what* and *how* we put it in that matters. It is well known that there are neural circuits that directly connect the gut to the brain, and that the gut is directly associated with the plasticity of brain cells and with our learning capabilities. Several gut hormones, or peptides, have been found to influence emotions, cognitive processes, and the capacity for acquiring new memories. The gut is known to serve as a second brain that has the capacity to 'feel' and 'know' certain things without necessarily analysing in a linear thought process. Hence, the importance of that 'gut feeling'. It is, thus, important to maintain a clean and healthy gut, not just for purely physical health but also for a healthy and alert mind.

Our food, physical exertion, and interaction with the environment have the potential to alter our brain health. What and how we eat has a significant impact on our cognitive capacities and protection of our brain cells. How we eat also impacts our general behaviour and response to circumstances and situations. As such, it is important to understand the difference between food and nutrition. Nutrients are necessary for biochemical reactions in our bodies. Our health and emotional responses depend on those. A loving and sensitive connection with the environment will naturally lead us to the ingestion of appropriate products.

When we only consume something that feels and tastes good, it is not necessary that the system will turn it into a substance that the body will absorb. Some other ingredients may be required to break it down and turn it into the subtler forms that nourish the trillions of minute cells in various parts of the body and the brain.

In today's lifestyle, where a great deal of stress is experienced by a large majority of people, several problems like indigestion and heartburn are commonly experienced. The body secretes certain biochemical substances as it creates a 'fight or flight' response in stressful situations. These secretions are garnered to alerting different bodily parts to cope with impending danger - be it a mentally stressful situation or a physical threat. They are generally hormones or other juices that lead the attention away from subtle inner processes, as all energy is diverted to the central motor system that alerts the muscles and limbs to cope with an external threat. They are garnered to dealing with stress than with processes like digesting and metabolizing food.

In times when the threat is external, these secretions get worked out in the process of fleeing or fighting, but when the threat is more mental or emotional in nature, the secretions may have a corrosive effect on the internal organs as they do not get expended through physical exertion.

It is, therefore, important that we give some thought to ourselves when we sit down to eat. A little observation of the mind and body, and a feeling of gratitude for the plate in front of us, helps to calm the system and bring the energies back to where they are required when we induct food into the body. It is not for nothing that traditionally we offered a thanksgiving before eating.

*Brahmarpanam brahma havi, brahmagnau brahmanahutam*
*'I offer to the sacred gastric fires that which has been produced by the cosmic fires of nature.'*

We do not have to necessarily chant a mantra before consuming food. All we need is to mentally collect ourselves for one moment before inducting life-giving nutrients into our systems.

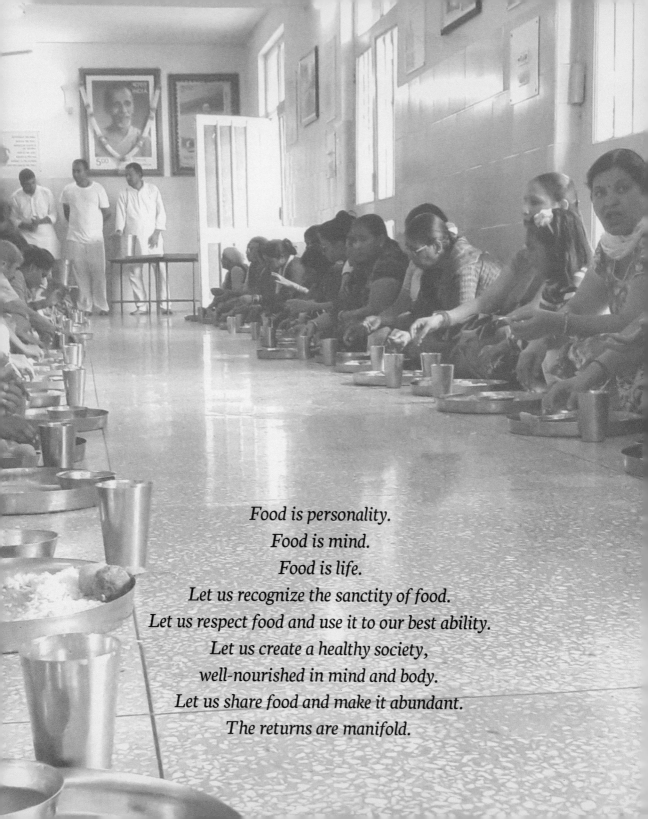

Food is personality.
Food is mind.
Food is life.
Let us recognize the sanctity of food.
Let us respect food and use it to our best ability.
Let us create a healthy society,
well-nourished in mind and body.
Let us share food and make it abundant.
The returns are manifold.

# Glossary

| | |
|---|---|
| ajwain | bishop's weed or carom |
| alsi | flax |
| amchoor | dried raw mango powder |
| amla | Indian gooseberry, considered a superfood in Ayurveda |
| | |
| bajra | pearl millet |
| baskeel | Himalayan bamboo shoot |
| bathua | *Chenopodium album*, commonly known as lamb's quarters or pigweed, is used as a food crop in many regions, while in some regions it is treated as just a weed. |
| bhang | hemp is a one strain of *Cannabis sattiva*. It grows wild in the lower Himalayan regions and is low on the psychoactive constituents with which cannabis is associated. |
| bhangjeera | beefsteak plant, *Perilla frutescens* |
| bhatt | Himalayan soyabean, usually black in colour. While being very nutritious, it is versatile and is used by the locals in a variety of ways. |
| boora | *tagar*, coarse sugar. *Tagar* or *boora* sugar is a porous sugar, which is made by melting sugar in water to reach a state of crystallization. This way, sugar loses its moisture and becomes 'clean'. It makes recipes more tasty. |
| | |
| chaulai | amaranth |
| chhuara | dried dates are a storehouse of vitamins, including vitamins A,C,E,K,B2, and B6. They can be used for savoury as well as sweet preparations. |
| chia | *Salvia hispanica*, often mistakenly called *sabja*. *Sabja* are tulsi seeds. As both originate in the mint family, they look similar. Both are superfoods. |
| chironji | Cuddapah almond, *Buchanania lanzan*. This lentil-sized seed of a deciduous tree that grows across India has a nutty, almond flavour and makes a good addition to many dishes. |
| chora | a fragrant woody bark that grows in the upper Himalayan regions. It adds flavour to daals and many vegetables. |

The sacred land—on the way to Badrinath